A TOOLBOX FOR SMALL CHURCHES

A Toolbox for Small Churches

A Spiritual and Practical Guide to Small Church Life

HILARY TAYLOR

THANKFUL BOOKS

Cover image and cartoons by Tim Charnick

Scriptures from the Holy Bible used in this book are
from the following translations:

New International Version (NIV) © 1973, 1978, 1984
    by International Bible Society.
Today's English Version (TEV) 1992 American Bible Society.
New Living Translation (NLT) Copyright 1996. Used by
    permission of Tyndale House Publishers Inc., Wheaton,
    Illinois 60189, USA. All rights reserved.
The Living Bible (TLB) owned by assignment by the Illinois Bank NA
    (as trustee). Used by permission of Tyndale House Publishers Inc.,
    Wheaton, Illinois 60189, USA. All rights reserved.
The Message (TM). Copyright Eugene H. Peterson, 1993, 1994, 1995.
    Used by permission of NavPress Publishing Group.
King James Version (KJV).

Book design and production for the publisher by
Bookprint Creative Services, <www.bookprint.co.uk>
Printed in Great Britain.

CONTENTS

ACKNOWLEDGEMENTS

Tade Agbesanwa	Custom House Baptist Church
Frank Brookes	Rayleigh Park Baptist Church
David Brownnut	Rhondda Baptist Network
Ron Buttery	Haddenham-cum-Dinton Baptist Church
Paul Collett	South London Tabernacle
Neil Coulson	Stapleton Baptist Church
Edith Dawson	Moss Side Church
Sally Fox	Crown Road Baptist Church
Aline Fynn	Hammersmith Christian Fellowship
Steve Gordon	Tasso Baptist Church
Catriona Gorton	Hugglescote Baptist Church
John Huffadine	New Basford Baptist Church
Sandra Kimber	Hampton Wick Baptist Church
Peter Leveson	Youth Co-ordinator, London Baptist Association
Stuart MacKay	Broadclyst Baptist Church
Penny Marsh	Royal Docks Community Church
Peter Osbourne	Yiewsley Baptist Church
Graham Parkinson	South West Baptist Association
David Priddy	Ashford Common Baptist Church
Bob Scott	Harlington Baptist Church
Norman Smith	Ashford Common Baptist Church
Richard Starling	East Dartmoor Baptist Church
David Sutcliffe	Sutton Bonington Baptist Church
Martin Taylor	Ashford Common Baptist Church

ACKNOWLEDGEMENTS

Sandra Thwaites	North Hanwell Baptist Church
Mark Turner	Barrow-on-Soar Baptist Church
Ken Walker	John Bunyan Baptist Church
Fiona Weatherhead	Hampton Baptist Church
Jan Williams	Haddenham-cum-Dinton Baptist Church
Nigel Williams	Canonbury Community Baptist Church

PREFACE

My mix of experience in churches, small and large, has given me a broad understanding of what it means to be church, but I am constantly being challenged as God always seems to be doing a new thing.

As I met people in my role in the Small Church Connexion in London, I was regularly asked to recommend resources particularly relevant for small churches. A number of good resources have been tried and tested and are listed in Chapter 9. However, not many books directly address the unique nature of small churches.

In 2004 as I was travelling on the underground into Central London, I was expressing my frustration to God about this, when I felt Him saying "Why don't you stop moaning and write one yourself?" This was not the response I was expecting!

I consulted several mature Christians who knew me and had worked with churches of different sizes and characters across the UK and they agreed that a resource specifically for small churches was needed. The book *Celebrating the Small Church* by Martin Robinson and Dan Yarnell published in 1993, which had encouraged many small churches, was no longer in print, and the majority of other books on the market had a different idea of what "small" meant. Many assume small is fewer than 125 members!

Two weeks after my call to write, I was invited to join a team called together by the Mission Department of the Baptist Union, to look at small churches nationally with the aim of providing better resources for them. This was an answer to prayer as it immediately gave me access to people who were passionate about small churches and who had years of personal hands-on experience.

I would like to thank Helen Beaven, Tim Charnick (for the great illustrations), Ken Hyde, Moira Kleissner, Peter Stockwell, Steve Mantle, Carol Murray, Martin Taylor, Nigel Williams, Ruth Wood and Dan Yarnell for their contributions to the text, as well as those who have read, edited and made suggestions over a number of months. Thanks also go to all the hardworking Ministers, Leaders and Officers in small churches listed in the Acknowledgements, who have been willing and delighted to write their stories to inspire and motivate us all into action.

Thanks also to the Small Church Connexion who are a great team of small church ministers charged with the task of encouraging the small churches across London. They have greatly inspired me during the "writing" season, as has the Regional Team of the London Baptist Association.

I am so grateful to those at my home church, Ashford Common Baptist Church, for encouraging me, praying for me and helping me to grow both as a person and as a Leader of the church.

Finally, special thanks go to my family who believed I could write this and encouraged me in many ways to carry on.

My prayer is that this book will help small churches to reach their potential to be all that God intended, fulfilling their mission to make Jesus known in their local community.

As William Carey said "Attempt great things for God. Expect great things from God".

FOREWORD BY DAN YARNELL

Wherever you travel throughout these islands, you will almost certainly find a small church. It is *the* normal expression of worship not only in the United Kingdom, or even in Europe, but right across the planet, and has been the normative experience of worship for most followers of Jesus since the early beginnings of the church.

Whenever you think of a small church, what word do you focus on? I often ask church leaders this question, and I have discovered that for many people, "small" is the obvious choice. For them "small" often implies failure, lacking what is needed to really succeed, or highly dependent on others with little or no life of its own.

In spite of the regular research that suggests that healthy smaller churches are often more effective in reaching the not-yet Christians, there is a great misconception that these smaller communities of faith are not really that important. You don't often hear the stories and ministries of these faith communities; they are just too ordinary and small. Even within leadership, many ministers begin in small churches but are almost expected to move to a larger church.

There is, however, good news for these faith communities. In our rapidly changing culture, there is a genuine renewed interest in smaller expressions of being church; from fresh and emerging expressions to home and house church experiences; from declining historic churches engaging more fully with their communities to specific people group experiences as well as church planting, the smaller church is not a failed large church, not an anomaly, but a genuine expression of being God's people in villages, towns and cities throughout the world.

That is one reason why I am very excited about this publication. I spent nearly twenty years working in and with small churches in the Midlands, and often wished there had been more resources to aid me in my leadership. There are of course some very good volumes on the smaller church coming from the States, yet there are few good resources here in the UK. I believe this important book fills a need for a more practical resource, which will be a great asset to anyone who is engaged in the life of a small church.

It is therefore a delight to recommend this important resource to you. Hilary Taylor writes from a place of compassion, of conviction and experience. This is not just a descriptive piece of writing; rather it is a genuine hands-on approach to the life and journey of working and worshipping in a smaller church.

As someone who has worked closely with her on the Baptist Union project looking at smaller churches, I know that this is not just a ministry but a God-given passion to assist smaller churches to fulfil their potential and become grace-filled, mission-directed expressions of God's lavish love to the world. Her continuing work in London networking smaller Baptist churches has given her a realistic perspective on the joys and struggles of leading and serving smaller churches.

For those who are daily living in the reality of the smaller church, this resource will certainly provide you with lots of practical encouragement and tools to assist you in your ministry and mission. For those who have not shared in this experience of being church, reading this might help you to understand and appreciate the valuable contribution many smaller churches are making here in these islands. Who knows, God may even challenge you to consider becoming part of this exciting journey.

Rev. Dan Yarnell, Lecturer, Birmingham Christian College,
Baptist Union
Specialist Mission Networker for Smaller Churches
Co-author (with Martin Robinson) of
Celebrating the Small Church;
author of Reaching People – The Small Church Approach

FOREWORD BY PAT TOOK

I am delighted to be able to recommend this resource for everyone who is engaged in the life of a small church.

Our Baptist origins are in congregations that were small enough to be able to covenant together in seriousness to walk together and watch over each other. Much of our churchmanship assumes that sort of intimacy and involvement on the part of all members.

However, the wider evangelical world has for many decades been shaped by large congregations and this has affected the identity and confidence of smaller congregations.

Too often the wealth that is to be found in these small communities is forgotten in the struggle to maintain buildings, programmes and mission agendas more appropriate to large churches. The laudable ambition to grow as a response to the gospel imperative can produce exhaustion and disillusionment when the strategies employed are beyond the capabilities of small congregations. But experience affirms that small communities are often the most effective at reaching people for Christ

Among the most positive and creative voices encouraging our small churches at the moment, Hilary Taylor has proved her worth, both in sharing in the leadership of a particularly effective congregation, and in leading the way in the London Baptist Association as we try to resource and celebrate the work of these little communities. This *Toolbox* she has produced will, I am sure, become an invaluable resource for everyone working in this demanding but rewarding area of Christian life.

Rev. Dr Patricia Took, Regional Minister,
London Baptist Association

HOW TO USE THIS BOOK

This book is designed to be read, dipped into, referred to and used as a collection of Tools.

It comprises 8 chapters divided into 3 sections. Each section is marked by symbols in the margin:

Book Each area of church work is earthed in Scripture, to remind us what God has called us to do for and with Him.

Camera Snapshots of real life as told by small churches around the UK

Spade These tools are designed to be used, photocopied and discussed. They are a selection of questions, practical suggestions, studies and checklists. They may well form the basis of a church action plan. However, they are not designed to replace prayer.

Chapter 9 is a list of resources based on the subject of each chapter and includes recommended books, websites and organisations to contact.

The Tools Sections from this book can also be found on the Baptist Union of Great Britain website www.baptist.org.uk for you to download.

Whilst most of the Snapshots and stories have been sourced from within the Baptist tradition, my friends and contacts in small churches within other traditions tell me that they face similar issues and are also interested in having tools. Consequently, I have tried to extend things where I have information. In particular, I have used the terms Local Team for local groupings of churches and Regional Team for wider groupings. So for example, the Local Team in the Methodist tradition would be the Circuit, in the Baptist tradition would be the District and in the Anglican tradition would be the Archdeacon's Area. The Regional Team in the Methodist tradition would be the District, in the Anglican tradition the Diocese and in the Baptist tradition would be the Association.

INTRODUCTION

It's 9:50am on a Sunday morning and the faithful few have turned up despite the rain. We do battle once more with the building's alarm system and gain entry. Within 20 minutes, the Youth Centre is transformed into a place to worship the Lord God Almighty himself. The church "kit" is kept in a cupboard for the week, everything from banners to coffee box, Sunday school books to overhead projector. The people begin to gather and greet each other with warmth and enthusiasm, ready for an encounter with the living God. Scripture is read, songs are sung, heartfelt prayers are shared aloud and participation is encouraged. God's Word is taken to heart and there is an opportunity for personal ministry. After the service, coffee is served, visitors are encouraged to return and the "church" is packed away until next week. Why do we do it? Because we believe God has brought us together to be a community, who worship together, learn together, laugh together, cry together, support each other and minister to each other: all 20 of us.

The small church *is* different, with restrictions on numbers of available people, money, abilities and so on, so it's just as well we know a big God with deep pockets. However, our small church wishes that there had been a "how to" manual for smaller churches when we were originally planted.

This *Toolbox* is designed to be just that. It is a manual that provides a Scriptural basis for the fundamentals of church life, such as worship, discipleship, fellowship and mission. There is a chapter on each of these topics with illustrations from small Baptist churches in the UK to identify with and take heart from, plus a practical selection of tools to work through and be the basis for an action plan.

We find many small churches in the New Testament being planted by Paul as he travelled around Asia Minor. As people became Christians, small groups met in homes:

> The churches in the province of Asia send you greetings. Aquila and Priscilla greet you warmly in the Lord, and so does the church that meets at their house. (1 Corinthians 16v19 NIV)

> Give my greetings to the brothers at Laodicea, and to Nympha and the church in her house. (Colossians 4v15 NIV)

The average home would not have accommodated more than roughly 20 people, though maybe Lydia's house in Thyatira was larger as she was a business woman of substance. Jesus' promise shows us that it is not about numbers, but His presence: ". . .where two or three come together in my name, there am I with them" (Matthew 18v20 NIV).

To quote Abraham Lincoln, "God must have loved small churches because he made so many of them."

A high percentage of Christians across the UK experience this valid expression of God's Kingdom every Sunday in congregations of 40 people or fewer. Out of about 2000 Baptist churches, approximately half of them are made up of churches with 40 or fewer members, distributed across each of the local Associations.

There are high numbers of small churches across the Christian denominations in the UK. The Church of England reported the adult average weekly attendance was less than 40 adults in approximately 47% of the 16,000 Parish churches in 2005.[1] The United

---

[1] Research and Statistics Department, Church House, London.

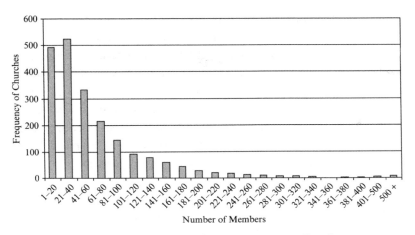

Distribution of Membership in UK Baptist Churches

Reformed and Methodist traditions also have many churches with 40 people or fewer.

There are various reasons why churches are small. Some are set in small rural communities while others have found a special mission among minority groups in large cities. Some are recent church plants or fresh expressions of church that have yet to grow or where growth is offset by people moving away. One has to be honest and recognise that some smaller churches, perhaps through lack of vision or fear of change, sadly are ready to die, or perhaps are in need of a re-birth. Yet others used to have many members but for various reasons numbers have declined. Going to church is no longer seen as important in our society, although the hunger for spirituality has increased over recent years. Sadly, many people now dismiss the church as one possible place to find the peace that eludes them.

There are also factors within a church, which could keep the numbers low. A high percentage of Christian young people leave home to attend university and higher education colleges, which removes the energy and dynamic input of the late teens and early twenties and many do not return home to work or live after education. Where several generations used to belong to the local church, jobs or high property prices now take away the sons and daughters of members, leaving an older and smaller congregation and fewer people to whom to pass the baton. Demographically the population is ageing so as church attendance reflects society in general, church membership will have aged and will continue to do so.

Many organisations, not just the churches have been affected by society's ambivalent attitude to commitment. Jobs, homes, relationships, clubs and voluntary organisations and churches are affected by this and they all find it difficult to fill essential posts and to inspire the necessary enthusiasm for the work. Added to this, people work hard for long hours or are on a shift pattern of work and at the end of a busy day, a church related meeting might be the last thing on their mind and Sunday may be the only day in the week left to relax. The breakdown of family life with children spending alternate weekends with Mum or Dad adds to the difficulty of establishing a pattern to the week.

All these factors and more need to be taken into account by churches and a way of working that fits each situation needs to be found.

In response to a Baptist Union questionnaire, 125 small churches across the UK when asked "What were the positives about being associated with a small church?" the following scored highly:

- Friendly atmosphere
- Everyone knows everyone
- Prayer needs can be shared quickly with people likely to understand them
- Pastoral support can be offered swiftly
- Opportunities for the willing to get involved
- Decisions can be made quickly and informally

(The lowest score in this section went to "Able to grasp mission opportunities quickly").

When asked "What were the negatives about being a small church?" the following were noted:

- Demands of legislation: Disability Discrimination Act / Child Protection
- Too few people to do things
- Restricted quality of music ministry
- Shortage of money
- Unsatisfactory building

Smaller churches need special people to lead them; ideally a "people person" who can inspire and persuade, rather than direct. Ministers of small churches are full-time, part-time or spare-time. Some have full time jobs or are bi-vocational, which helps the bills, those of the church and the pastor, to be paid. Leadership is a complex and often thankless task, so a chapter in this manual is dedicated to those issues with helpful hints on how to survive.

A small church is not a smaller sized version of a large church. One church learned this lesson the hard way. In 1983, a church of 100 members planted a church 2 miles away in an empty Church of England building. In those days, there was no training for church planting, so the 20 pioneers just had to get on with it. Three of the men with full-time jobs had been deacons and were now plunged in at the deep end to lead a new church with little outside help. Most of the new congregation had large church experience so were happy to put together programmes and meetings, special services and leaflet deliveries, but after a few years, they were all worn out. They needed help which came from a worker in the Mission Department of the London Baptist Association. The church was trying to behave like a large church but with fewer people. He suggested that they close all activities except Sunday services for a while and have a good rest. The members then realised that a small church is not a small version of a big one, it's a different animal altogether.

Sound familiar? Sad to say, this mistake is being made all over the UK resulting in tired and ineffective people. One of the Devil's tactics is to wear us out so we can't be involved in God's business. God needs strong, alert soldiers on the front line. Every small church is an expression of Christ in a specific location, usually with a specific task.

The message that a small church is not the same thing as a scaled down large church (even if some actually had been much larger at some point in their history) must be heard loud and clear. There is an assumption that a church of, say, 70–100 members is a typical sized church and that a church of 30 or 40 members should therefore be regarded as an emaciated version of this "normal" model. The complaint is heard "we can't do as much as a larger church, or as much as we used to". While this may be true, it is emphatically not the point. Small churches are no more designed to do all that large churches do any more than the family saloon car is designed to do the work of a bus. However, this mindset is deeply entrenched and needs to be challenged. If leaders and members of small churches could genuinely feel that their church with 40 members or less has integrity and a dynamic of its own rather than being a pale imitation of a large church, that could be immensely liberating. Along with this message goes the need to say to small churches: "Play to your strengths".

There are often factors present that cause hope to fade in a small church, such as low numbers of committed people, months without visitors, or no new converts or baptisms (the sowers need to realise they may not see the harvest). Some congregations are getting older and lacking energy and others are small, having once been large and fondly remember the "good old days". Being prepared to think radically is often required and solutions can be found to produce growth instead of decline.

The task of teaching and nurturing children and young people in their faith in a small church is a difficult one. Most of the teaching aids are aimed at large classes of children of a similar age, with a fun collection of illustrative games, which often need teams of 3 or more children! The task of the small church teacher is therefore magnified, as they have to prepare a lesson while adapting everything to their particular group, often with large age gaps. The parameters of the Safe to Grow policy also present a challenge for a small church where the numbers are limited. There is a chapter that deals with such issues and offers some practical suggestions. It is important to include the children and young people in the life of the church and encourage their faith. They are not just the church of tomorrow, they are an important part of the church of today!

Large or old buildings owned by small churches can be both a blessing and a curse, especially listed buildings where change can be restricted. However, many churches have thought imaginatively about their buildings and now use them for community use or hire the space to outside companies. Ideas for this are included in a later chapter and help with funding can be found in Chapter 9.

To support smaller churches in their work, Small Church Networks are emerging in the UK to locally address issues that arise and to provide resources and general help. Contact your geographical area team for details of your local network.

Information is good. However, for the church of the living God, direction for a specific group of people, in a specific place at a specific point in time, can only come from the Father himself. The church needs to follow the instructions in 2 Chronicles 7v14: "If my people, who are called by my name, will humble themselves and pray and seek my face and turn from their wicked ways, then I will hear from heaven and forgive their sin and will heal their land" (2 Chronicles 7v14 NIV).

We need to make prayer a top priority, as communication with God is vital. We need to be a listening, humble people. We need direction and encouragement from the King of kings so we need to constantly seek His face. We are called to be holy and turn our back on our "wicked ways". We need to live lives worthy of the name "Christian".

CHAPTER ONE

WORSHIP

"For where two or three come together in my name, there am I with them."
(Matthew 18v20 NIV)

Personal Worship

Worship is a response to God, motivated by love not duty. An expression of love that can be quiet or exuberant, desperate or extravagant. It can be in our native language or in an unlearnt language, it can be active or still. But having the amazing privilege of being called by name into God's very presence should ensure that we always come humbly and on our knees. If we each get our personal worship on the right track, the corporate experience of worship is more likely to honour God, even if we are few in number.

Biblical Expressions of Worship

We read about a variety of worship styles in the Bible, from the people of Israel worshipping God in a tent in the desert, to King David praising unreservedly through the city streets, to worship in the great temple, to wise men bowing in awe before the manger, to an active and practical infant church. We can learn from these examples and many others woven through the Scriptures that worship is about hearts and lives, not music, ritual and words.

David, a great musician and poet, wrote many of the psalms in which he expresses the various facets of his relationship with God. Some are adoration to a King, some thanks to a protector and provider. Some voice his amazement at creation and the creator, some describe his Saviour. Some are written from exasperation and some are recognition of his own failings.

Worship is a Lifestyle

When we stop and consider the immensity of what God the Father has done on our behalf through Christ's sacrifice on the cross, worship is our only response. We owe Him our very lives, every minute of every day. When we come to Christ, He gives us a new start, a clean slate through forgiveness, a new set of rules to live by that challenges the world's values, and the constant presence of the Holy Spirit to guide us. Worship is a twenty-four hour, seven days a week lifestyle. God is worshipped (or not) through our every action, word and thought.

As the wise men came to worship the new-born King bringing their gifts to Him, so we too should bring our gifts, not only our natural talents and spiritual gifts, but also our resources – money, time, energy and availability. We may feel that we have very little to offer both personally and as a small church, but for some reason, God chooses the weak to show His glory to the world. He chooses to love the world through us, His church, and those parts that are small in number are included as His vehicle to love the nations.

Putting God First

Worship is putting God at the centre of your life, living His way ("to act justly and to love mercy and to walk humbly with your God" Micah 6v8 NIV) and keeping the Great Commandment:

> One of them, an expert in the law, tested him with this question: "Teacher, which is the greatest commandment in the Law?" Jesus replied: " 'Love the Lord your God with all your heart and with all your soul and with all your mind.' This is the first and greatest commandment. And the second is like it: 'Love your neighbour as yourself.' All the Law and the Prophets hang on these two commandments." (Matthew 22v35–40 NIV)

We also find in the Bible warnings about worshipping anything else but God himself. In some parts of the world, bowing down and worshipping man made statues or other objects is a way of life. In Isaiah 44, the prophet is very scathing about man made idols. In UK society today, there are other substitutes. Idols are anything that we place ahead of God as a priority such as a job, people, car, football, beauty, money, fashion, health, or our homes. Even doing things in the church. All of these things may be good in themselves, if held in proper perspective, but if that perspective is not God's perspective, we end up prioritising wrongly.

> In church, we must be careful as sometimes we can be busy being busy, and focus on "the work of the Lord", instead of "the Lord of the work".

The way we live is not only observed by God, but also watched closely by people around us. We look to each other for examples of how to live, and in a small church, this can be both helpful and discouraging, as we know each other well, warts and all. We are all on different stages of the Christian journey and those newer in the faith tend to look at the older Christians for an example. This is good until you realise they are expecting perfection!

Worshipping in the Wilderness

Each of us has days when life is filled with unexpected shock, or tragedy, when things happen that make us ask "Why?" We may feel that God has abandoned us and the last thing we want to do is worship Him. God knows that we have dark days so in His word are examples of people like us going through troubles when the doubts come and questions are left unanswered. In Psalm 13, we read of despair:

> How long, O LORD? Will you forget me for ever? How long will you hide
> your face from me? How long must I wrestle with my thoughts and every
> day have sorrow in my heart? How long will my enemy triumph over me?
> (Psalm 13v1–2 NIV)

Yet if we read on, there is an offering of praise and worship as the writer once more turns to focus on God, not his problem: "But I trust in your unfailing love; my heart rejoices in your salvation. I will sing to the LORD, for he has been good to me" (Psalm 13v5–6 NIV).

On dark days like this, we may not want to go to church at all, but feel as there are so few people, we are duty bound to turn up. This may be the best thing as a touch from God or prayer from others may be just what is needed. A lot of songs or hymns we sing in our services are of praise and adoration, about the cross and our faith in Jesus. There are not many heart cries to God that break through the pain, trusting our great God to bring us through. We need to be real in our worship and cry to Him as David did many times in the psalms.

Corporate Worship

In a grey Welsh valleys town, an elderly lady unlocks the heavy wooden doors of a huge chapel, built during the revival to seat up to 1000 worshippers. Gradually another 10 ladies (average age 70+) gather in the echoing sanctuary, finding their usual pews and settling onto assorted cushions brought in to ease the hardness of the seats. They chat to each other, sharing their problems and worries, enjoying fellowship, which for most of them began when they were in Sunday School together 60 years ago. By the time the visiting Lay Preacher arrives and is taken into the vestry for a word of prayer, the congregation is complete as a couple of men and 2 children have arrived. The preacher looks out over a congregation scattered among the pews, some barely visible at the back, others smiling encouragingly near the front. The service unfolds – hymn singing, prayer, a good sermon, then a chance to chat again before the chapel is closed up for another week.

Corporate worship has as many expressions as there are churches. All are valid as long as God is central. Each church is unique so the expression of worship together should not be a copy of the church down the road. Orderly not chaotic worship is recommended in the New Testament, but within structure, there must be room for the Holy Spirit to inspire and provoke a response from us.

If you have worshipped in a crowd of 10,000 or even 100, you notice the difference when there are only 10 in your small church. Is it the lack of volume when people sing? Is it that you know that the speaker can see you and people can hear you sing? We in small churches can worry immensely about our worship times, particularly when we are fewer in number than usual. However, because of the close relationships, people may feel freer to pray aloud about how life is and know that each is supported by the others. There is often a depth of intimacy during worship times with God and each other when the numbers are smaller.

Together, seek God's face as well as His hands

Prayers of supplication (asking) and petition are part of our worship, as is intercession on behalf of our community, town, nation and world but it is important to seek God's face as well as His hands. To have time and space to seek God together as church is an important part of worship. Sharing what God is saying through a scripture, picture or word that is brought during worship, enables God's direction to be jointly owned by the whole church.

Each Person Contributing

There is something special about the church coming together to celebrate who God is, His goodness and His activity in our lives during the week. Worshipping the Father, Son and Holy Spirit should be an active experience with everyone bringing a contribution, according to Paul: "What then shall we say, brothers? When you come together, everyone has a hymn, or a word of instruction, a revelation, a tongue or an interpretation. All of these must be done for the strengthening of the church" (1 Corinthians 14v26 NIV).

Practically, everyone contributing something is easier in a smaller church. In a large church it becomes impractical for everyone to bring a hymn, a sermon or a revelation. It would simply take more hours than there are in the day. Compromises to this scriptural ideal have to be made because of sheer weight of numbers. In a small church everyone is valued and their contribution is accepted and encouraged. It is also appreciated that for some people, just getting to church and sitting and receiving is all they can do. Their situation is known and they are still valued.

Taking part is much less daunting in a small church. Praying out loud, reading a scripture from the front, playing an instrument in public – all are easier when there are only 10 people in front of you than it would be if faced by 100 or 1000.

It is easier to take risks in a small church. Allowing someone to preach or do a solo for the first time is an easier decision to take if there are only 10 people who might be disappointed or upset if it is not actually the gifting of the individual on show.

> There have been times in our small church where the climate of contributing, having been established, encouraged some visitors to feel comfortable in asking awkward questions of the preacher when he was in full flight!

Service Leaders

The service leader can be either a member of the congregation or the preacher. In a small church, spreading the responsibility for worship across a number of people enables an outworking of the scripture in 1 Peter 2v9 and Revelation 1v6. Whoever leads should not only have a heart for worship, but also a heart of compassion for the people, and be sensitive to how they have come. The service leader should be personally prepared to worship and have a service framework to work to. However any framework should be flexible so the Holy Spirit can move.

On some days, the congregation arrives with joy and is ready to celebrate. On other days, there is a heaviness that pervades the room making it really hard to worship. Hebrews 13v15 describes this situation as a "sacrifice of praise" because it is the last thing you want to do. It is a real sacrifice of self to God, who is worthy of praise no matter how we feel and what kind of a week we've had. We need to be lifted above our problems (which are "me" centred) and be drawn into God's presence and focus on Him. From this position, we often find our perspective changing and having been reminded of how great and able God is, we see our problems on the real scale, and are often in a place to see solutions. In a smaller church, there may be one or two people whose mood will dominate the atmosphere. On a heavy day, the service leader has to decide whether to just stop and pray in response to the heaviness, or give opportunity for burden sharing and praying for the person or situation, before continuing.

Music

Music has traditionally played a major role in our worship to God. The great hymns based on Scripture have much to teach us and are still being discovered by new Christians singing them for the first time. It is important to regularly affirm your organist, pianist or music team as they do work hard behind the scenes on a weekly basis. If there is only one musician in the church, be mindful that they need to have a regular week off and just be free to worship without the pressure of playing.

The Sermon

It is a challenge to bring a fresh message each week to teach and encourage people no matter where they are on their journey with God.

> A small church leader writes: A tutor at College taught us a valuable lesson about not skimping on sermon preparation just because we knew there would only be 2 or 3 people in the congregation. He said "You should always preach to 1 as if you are preaching to 100, and preach to 100 as if you are preaching to 1". The quality of the message should never depend on the size of the congregation.

A sermon can be set more closely to the level of the hearers in a small church because relationships can be built, and a better knowledge of individuals gained. At the same time, care must be taken not to allow knowledge of someone's personal situation to creep out into the sermon text. Making someone feel embarrassed in public is not usually a helpful approach. Care must be taken not to constantly put across the message that the people are not good enough or there is a lot in their lives still to sort out. Someone once commented that they were fed up with going to church to be told off, while those who never went got away with it! Farmers wisely only shear their sheep once a year and preachers must follow the example. Following the command to "feed my lambs and feed my sheep" issued to Peter (John 21v15–17), we must help people to read and love God's word. Lambs are fed by picking them up, tucking them under your arm and gently bottle-feeding. Sheep are led to safe pasture and told to eat the grass. There are many "sheep" still being fed like "lambs" in our churches i.e. only getting what is prepared for them and not reading the Bible for themselves. We must ensure that personal Bible reading and study is taking place by giving out daily notes or showing how to use a concordance or study Bible. Bear in mind the mixture of lambs and sheep in the congregation as you prepare the message.

It can be disheartening when an inspired message is preached and no one can remember much about it soon afterwards. It is always good to remind yourself that: "The word that I speak, it will not fail to do what I plan for it; it will do everything I send it to do" (Isaiah 55v11 TEV).

A good question to ask yourself is "What did I have for dinner last Tuesday?" Chances are that you cannot remember, but you know that it did you good! So it is with the Word of God.

How People Learn

Educationalists state that we remember:

20% of what we read	30% of what we hear
40% of what we see	50% of what we say
60% of what we do	90% of what we see, hear, say and do

In an average group, there are different learning styles:

20% of people are auditory, listeners	40% of people learn from visual images
40% of people are tactile, movers and doers	

(Figures from www.soton.ac.uk/studentsupport)

In a small church it is even more important to take notice of such advice because we need people to progress quickly from depending on milk to being able to take solid food. We need to shorten the recovery times of those who come to us spiritually ill. We need those young in the faith to mature rapidly because we need their (mature) help in the overall ministry of the church.

Sundays at South London Tabernacle by Paul Collett, Pastor

I am standing in the stillness of Sunday morning looking at the empty chairs that have been set out in neat rows by Dorrie our 90-year-old deacon the night before. I pick a chair and visualise who may be sitting there in a couple of hours. I pray for them and their family. Other faces come to mind, parents and children at the local school, neighbours, some who think of us as "their church" though they rarely come.

I love this time of quiet renewal. I feel the compassion and grace of Jesus reaching out to gather in his people. I feel the struggle and the anger of Jesus as he mourns our brokenness and pain.

By 10.00am I am in the office finishing off final preparation for the service. Carol shouts "Good morning" as she comes in to set out the PA and keyboard. We share news of the week. I return to the manse to get breakfast and join Carole my wife in the mayhem of getting our children ready.

At 10.30am 11-year-old Zakhaan knocks. He has come to help operate the midi files and OHP. We cross the road to the church and find Herolin there with Beck setting up for Sunday School. Two other children have already arrived and everyone wants to work the OHP. We agree whose turn it is, and work together putting out Bibles and hymn books.

It's 10.50am. I am determined to start on time today! Only six adults are here. Dorrie and Elsie join me for a prayer.

By 11.00am the congregation has grown to 10 adults and 8 children. We start the service with songs. More people trickle in. By the time we get to the notices, we have 20 adults and 15 children and young people.

At 12.10pm the service concludes with the grace (words are on the OHP for those who don't know them) and after a minute of quiet, a friendly buzz of conversation begins. I stand by the door, but only two people leave. Teas, coffees and cake are handed around by Inumidun and Heidi, two of our young people. I am served while talking to Attila, a Hungarian here for the second week running. It's fun but hard work. I try to listen carefully to what is said and what is not said as I make my way around the groups of chatting people. I scribble short notes to myself about anything important.

By 1.30pm finally everything is packed away and checked. We walk back across the road. I feel a mixture of elation and relief and I am deeply grateful to God for what he is doing in us through Jesus.

The Blessings and Problems of Worship in a Small Church by Sally Fox, Crown Road Baptist Church, Sutton, Surrey

Worship can be both inspiring and limiting in a small congregation. At Crown Road Baptist Church in Sutton, we have a congregation that could be as many as 20 but is usually not more than 15. One of the big problems of a small church is that it only takes a few to be absent and the congregation can be very small indeed. Because the church is small, they have me as their Lay Pastor on a part-time basis. While this is a good arrangement, I sometimes feel that a part-time pastor makes everyone feel it is a part-time church and so regular attendance is not part of their expectations.

Just occasionally we do have a bigger congregation. Recently we have had church parades, 'baby blessings' and 'marriage blessings' all of which have brought lots of people to church. These occasions have brought blessings and problems of their own. Many people have come with no idea about "churchiness" and have been pleasantly surprised that it can be enjoyable. We regulars have got excited and spent our Bible Study prayer time on a Monday praying for them all but sadly, none of our happy visitors seem willing to repeat the experience so we continue to be a small congregation.

My experience as pastor tells me that singing in a very small gathering can be very difficult, so I say, "we need 6 to sing" – but it really does depend which 6 are present. But what exciting and adventurous things can be done in a small church. Due to our relaxed flexibility in our multipurpose hall, we can occasionally do things that would be totally impossible for a larger congregation.

About once a year we do "parachute games". A parachute or play-chute is a great way to get people out of their seats and active for a while. With our parachute we have acted out Bible stories (the story of Jonah and the stilling of the storm were very good for this). We symbolically prayed our prayers of praise, intercession and confession (prayers are written on small pieces of paper, screwed up and the papers bounced on the chute while singing suitable songs).

Sitting round a small table for communion makes the whole service very much more intimate and prayerful (about 12 is the maximum I would consider for this). Using a formal liturgy is not a very Baptist activity but in a small group where individuals can read the parts, it can bring a great sense of involvement. There is lots of beautiful worship material available; the Wild Goose Worship Group of the Iona Community being one of many useful sources. Dramatic readings and short plays are also useful. These don't need to be rehearsed; I just give out the scripts and allocate the parts and most people rise to the occasion.

Open prayer can be a blessing and a problem. Some people seem to feel they have to say as much as possible to make up for lack of numbers and this can take away any sense of prayerfulness from the others. I would like to encourage more times of silence but many people really seem to be uncomfortable with this and will try to fill the space with anything and everything whether it is relevant or not.

Interactive sermons happen from time to time whether planned or not. Because the group is small and everyone knows each other fairly well, people feel very relaxed and so feel able to make comments or ask questions without any encouragement on my part. This can be very interesting and very irritating both for me as the preacher and for other members of the congregation. As we have quite a few visiting preachers, due to my part-time status, I always warn them not to ask questions unless they really want an answer; rhetorical questions are not taken rhetorically in my small church.

We are a small church for worship on a Sunday but during the week we are often bursting at the seams. On Tuesdays, as many as 80 people ranging in age from a few weeks to a few decades come to our Parent and Toddler groups. Everyone has the opportunity to hear the Gospel in the form of a short Bible story; and most of them take the option. On Thursdays about 20 boys come for Boys' Brigade and on Fridays about 40 girls come for Girls' Brigade. All of them hear the gospel in a way that is suitable for their age and development. These three groups are important to our church life and all but 2 of the 12 people who work within them are members of the church fellowship.

In all churches, whether big or small, some days are great and some days are difficult but every day is a gift from God and we try to use all his gifts according to His generosity.

WORSHIP TOOLS

Questions

This is a list of questions to help to review what happens in your church relating to Worship and will hopefully stimulate discussion between the Leadership, Worship Leaders and Musicians.

Service Leaders

How do we encourage our small congregation to prepare to worship God together on a Sunday?
Encourage the congregation to come at least 10 minutes before the service starts, just to sit and prepare themselves for worship. Playing suitable music is helpful. A common problem in a small church is that when people arrive, they want to chat about how the week has been because of the relationship with most of the others there. If left unchecked, this can distract those who want to be quiet, and they themselves have not had time to sit and focus. In cases like this, it may be necessary for the person leading the worship to prepare the congregation for worship within the time of the service.

How do the service leader/musician/s prepare to worship on a Sunday? Do they pray together?
If the service leader is in-house and not a musician, invite them to join the musician/s when practising the list of songs, and pray together. If the service leader is a visitor, invite them to pray with the musicians before the service.

Is there liaison between the service leader and preacher?
The preacher can provide a subject or verse on which the service leader can focus in the singing/prayer time. In many cases, the subject and text of the message is unknown, so the service leader prays and waits for direction from God. Despite all the unknowns and uncertainties, the Holy Spirit can weave it all together beautifully.

Is the congregation encouraged to worship in their quiet times at home using CDs, Christian radio, God Channel etc?

Make sure your small church is informed about the Christian radio/TV stations/web sites. It is helpful to have a library of worship tapes or CDs to lend to people to play during the week, but is much better if they buy their own.

Help for new Service Leaders?

For those who are new to leading services, a good framework to start with is helpful. Here are 2 suggestions to give the service balance:

ACTS

Adoration, Confession, Thanksgiving and Supplication ('asking' prayers)

PATHS

Praise, Admitting (confession), Thanksgiving, Hearing (listening to God) and Supplication (asking prayers)

Both of these frameworks will include prayers, hymns/songs, notices, offering, children's talk, and listening to God. The leader then has to decide where in the framework to place the sermon and/or communion. Encourage your service leaders by arranging a TIMMs module called Preparing Sunday (See Chapter 9 for details).

Music

Has the style of music been agreed? Hymns/songs/chants/choral etc or a mixture? Are the hymns valued for their content of Scripture or is there pressure to just use new songs?

This can be a contentious issue, so agreement between service leaders and the musician/s is vital. Most churches use a variety of styles and genres.

Are the church copyright licences up to date?
Most songs are legally copyright and many licences are available to churches from the Christian Copyright Licensing (Europe) Ltd. Details in Chapter 9. Of course, value for money needs to be considered. If you only occasionally use songs on an OHP or printed sheet, is it worth the words-copy licence?

Decide to use books or acetates for an overhead projector or laptop/projector.
See section on Technology.

Are the songs/hymns children friendly?
If you have children attending regularly, find some songs that have actions and are easy to learn and repetitive etc.

If you are blessed with several musicians, are there sufficient music resources available for each of them?
E.g. a book each or licensed photocopies.

Is the congregation involved in making music?
Percussion lends itself to participation.

Does your church own any instruments and are they insured?
E.g. organ, piano, keyboard.

Musicians

A heart for worship is far more important than musical ability. The musician/s must also have a heart for God's people, not just be good/ok musician/s or singers.

Are new people encouraged to share their musical ability within the church? Is there encouragement to attend training days or conferences for service leaders or musician/s?
Put the church onto helpful mailing lists such as Kingsway and keep up to date with latest events (see Chapter 9).

39

Music Groups

Does the group rehearse and pray together on a regular basis?
Weekly is ideal, though not always practical. You can never lead further than you have gone yourself. Practice doesn't actually make perfect – but it does help!

Does the group have a defined leader?
Each team needs a leader to co-ordinate and encourage the rest.

Have you discussed if non-Christians can join the music group? What are your thoughts on this issue?

Common Issues About Worship and Some Answers

We don't have anyone with musical ability, so we can't do worship

> A small church in Surrey borrow musicians from their local Churches Together group on a rota. A pianist or guitarist makes all the difference to them, and demonstrates that Churches Together can have practical value.

- A suggestion is to approach a local school, college or university and ask if any music students would like to play in the church. A small church in London currently has a Russian music student playing at their services.
- Accompanying singing in worship is more about the confidence to keep going despite mistakes, than it is about musical excellence.
- Many of our churches have a high proportion of older people. In times past, before TV, a large number of people learnt the piano as a child, and singing round the piano was a popular pastime. So probably 1 in 3 of your older people used to play. So get them ALL to take turns one day. You will have to set their expectations

correctly and make it fun – but you will be surprised at the hidden talent.

- How much musical ability do you really need?

> There is a story about some monks who always sang loudly, but seriously out of tune. Then they got the opportunity of having a day led by a world famous tenor. He made their worship songs sound glorious, absolutely beautiful. They thought God would be so impressed. But next day, the Lord said to the Abbot "I didn't hear any worship yesterday. What happened?"

- See the Worship without Music section.

We don't have anyone to lead worship (or I lead the worship as well as doing everything else)

If you have a church, you have people who want to worship. Give everyone the job of planning a service (and if you only have a congregation of 10, and you might also be able to persuade most of them to stand up and lead). Give help to those who need it. Give everyone lots of encouragement for stepping up to the mark and giving it a go. Try again some time later. After 2 attempts, get those who showed some gifting to lead on a more regular basis on a rota. The more often they try, the easier it gets. People are often more comfortable leading in a team so persuade a housegroup to lead together, each taking part.

It is hard to get consistency in developing worship because we have so many different visiting speakers.

Stop getting your visiting speakers to lead the whole service. Get them to concentrate on the sermon. Do the rest of the service in-house, and develop your service leaders.

> To have a balanced diet of Scripture in a situation where there are many visiting preachers, it is useful to write a preaching plan for each season and communicate it to the preachers! It is also helpful to have sermon recordings from a local small or large church handy in case of those moments when the preacher cannot come at short notice.

We have an elderly congregation. I want to encourage them into modern ways of worship, but I don't want to upset them.
If they love singing hymns, slowly over time introduce some of the more modern hymns. Encourage a few people to read the Scripture aloud or to choose a hymn and say why they love it.

For people who find speaking aloud daunting, an opportunity to write a prayer and have it read from the front by someone else or simply attaching it to a cross while quiet music is played is a good way of contributing.

So what are the strengths of a smaller group in worship?
The most obvious one would seem to be in the area of communion. Where ten or twenty people come together around the Lord's Table, they can do that very simply and meaningfully as a genuine family in close relationship with one another. Other strengths are having many people able to contribute in the service and people happier to share their prayer needs with the whole group.

Ideas and Suggestions

Worshipping God Together Without Music

Have you thought about exploring other expressions of worship, or do you rely on songs/hymns?
Here are some suggestions:

- Prayer – spontaneous prayers out loud or in small groups or silently.
- Praise out loud at the same time.

- Reading the Bible together aloud especially Psalms.
- Writing your own psalm is an excellent way of expressing your thoughts and feelings towards God.
- Meditation on Scripture.
- Dramatic reading of Scripture.
- Preaching is part of worship – it should not be regarded as separate.
- Each person bringing a word, reading, prayer or testimony.
- Have a quiet corner where there is a collection of smooth stones that people can pick up and use to focus on milestones in their lives where God has touched them significantly, or meditate on God being our rock.
- Have a candle burning and encourage people to share thoughts about Jesus being light of the world.
- If your tradition encourages the use of spiritual gifts, consider how to include them (prayers for healing, tongues, prophecy etc).

Some of the Active Worship suggestions (see below) can also be used without music, too.

Use of CDs

If you are not blessed with musicians, consider investing in backing tracks on CD or MP3 files – hymns/songs especially recorded for people to sing along to. Watch out for the introduction and the right place to start singing!

> The leader at a small Baptist Church in Berkshire bought a set of worship CDs, and used those whenever there was no one to play an instrument. As a visitor, it was a bit weird, with your eyes closed, you were in the heavenlies, worshipping with angels. When you opened your eyes, you sometimes came down to earth with a bump being reminded that there were less than 20 people present.

You do need a person dedicated to this task who is prepared to get the hymn/song list from the service leader during the week and find the appropriate recordings. They have to have a selection of CDs, find the songs and put them on during the service at the right moment and be as seamless as possible. There are several collections of popular songs and hymns on CD, or digital hymn resource (see Chapter 9). They are helpful if your lone musician is on holiday, ill or would just like a week off.

Active Worship

- Use of art e.g. pictures on a screen behind song words, scrolling pictures while music plays, being creative with paint, pastels, charcoal, choosing pictures and writing a Bible verse onto them.
- Use of body – express your worship to God in a variety of positions: stand, sit, kneel, lay prostrate, hands reaching out, jump, shout, dance, clap. (Use a concordance to research how scriptural these different expressions are.)
- Drama or Mime – actions often speak louder than words – act out Bible stories.
- Dance.
- Use of flags, streamers, banners.
- Using objects to look at or pass round to enhance worship e.g. a variety of crosses.
- Writing down problems or prayers of intercession and putting them at the foot of the cross.
- Writing down sins and nailing them to a wooden cross.
- Foot or hand washing.
- Prayer walking.

Special People, Special Needs

Small churches often attract people who have special needs in some area. Here are some suggestions to enhance their worship experience.

Seeing – large print on sheets (or sit at the front to see screen and speakers clearly), Braille books & Bibles.

Hearing – if you have your own premises, consider installing a hearing induction loop, or encourage individuals to sit at the front (maybe offer them more comfortable chairs also as a reward for being on the front line). It can be helpful if speakers use microphones (but note comments below re technology).

Mobility – room for wheelchairs (not as a back row), chairs with arms for those who need that extra help in sitting and standing.

Learning Difficulties – use of pictures in the sermon, storytelling style, visual aids.

Culture

- Use the rich diversity of different people groups in the church e.g. have an African day with traditional dress, African preacher, songs in native language, food etc.
- Use a worship style to suit the congregation, but you can't please all the people all the time (Don't hit the lowest common denominator trying).
- Watch for clashes of church culture, as it can be a problem (traditional v. new) – God's culture of peace and forgiveness is needed!

It is advised that any changes be made gradually, with explanations of what and why they are happening.

Technology

- If it can go wrong, it will go wrong, and always at the most awkward moment. Only employ electronic aids when you have a trained operator. This may well be a young person and it may be just the introduction to involvement in church life and worship that they need. Encourage them in turn to train others. Technology is not essential, particularly in a small church but should be considered when it could enhance the service (Small churches can sometimes feel under pressure to have it).

- Illustrations – Pictures on laptop/projector can helpfully illustrate the sermon or songs. However, they need to be to the point, and must enhance rather than take away. If the congregation are watching the screen, they will not be paying attention to the speaker! Video/DVD clips can be effective, but you need an up-to-date licence.

- PA Equipment – If there are more than 30 in your congregation, or your music team uses amplified equipment, you may require microphones/PA. Check the sound levels will suit the building. If the building is not owned by the church, there may be a PA installed already. May you use it? Otherwise, a portable PA can be used or an agreement reached with the owner to install equipment. If using portable PA, is there storage space?

- If there are only a small number of people in a large room, encourage them to sit close together. It is more practical than using PA equipment.

CHAPTER TWO

FOLLOWING AND SERVING JESUS WHOLEHEARTEDLY

To be totally sold out to the Lordship of Jesus means doing what He says and going where He says, when He says. Is it inconvenient? Often. Is it costly? Usually. Will it bring pain? Sometimes. But is it worth it? ALWAYS!
(Sue Prosser, Destined for the Deep*)*

Discipleship is vital in a Small Church

If there are fewer of you, you need everyone to put their hand to the plough. Every pair of hands is essential to keep a small church going. Every effort needs to be made to ensure that the faithful few are discipled to be the best followers of Christ they can be. True, some do not have the abilities or endurance of others, but we need everyone to work together, shoulder to shoulder. We need to encourage each other to "keep on keeping on". A small body needs to take care to have every limb working as well as it can.

Keep The Cross Central

At the cross, an amazing exchange took place. Jesus' life for mine. Forgiveness is available, a new beginning is possible and eternal life is secured. Knowing what you believe, whom you believe in and why, are basic truths that keep us steady, like roots that hold plants in the ground. They keep us stable, especially when the going gets tough and we need to stay focused on the cross at all times. Daily nourishment from God through his Word, prayer and fellowship are essential to our development. As our relationship with God and our understanding of God increase, growth takes place and living like Christ becomes easier.

Freedom

One of the most important early steps as a Christian is to unload the baggage brought from the past. If not unloaded, it weighs heavily and affects both the present and the future. The change that occurs when people embrace that freedom affects the whole of our church life. The exciting change is noticed by all and others realise that they need the same freedom. There are courses (see Chapter 9) that enable deeper understanding about our position in Christ (read Ephesians Chapter 1) and how freedom from the past is possible. It is essential that these deep foundations are laid in every Christian's life.

Following Jesus

> Just as you trusted Christ to save you, trust him, too, for each day's problems; live in vital union with him. Let your roots grow down into him and draw up nourishment from him. See that you go on growing in the Lord, and become strong and vigorous in the truth you were taught. Let your lives overflow with joy and thanksgiving for all he has done. (Colossians 2v6–7 TLB)

Discipleship is the process of following Jesus and requires obedience and perseverance. It's not an easy option but it is the best way to live. It involves learning that everything we have comes from Him and we must to hold our possessions in open hands, not a tight grip.

To be in the centre of God's will with His constant presence to guide, protect and illuminate is an adventure, but at a cost. The first disciples chose to give up their agendas and old lives to follow Jesus in response to His call to take up their cross and follow Him.

For those called to smaller churches, this call may mean leaving behind the benefits of a large church – familiar Christian networks, many hands to do the work, worship led by a band etc. But God calls and gathers people with various gifts who will work together to fulfil his purposes and respond to the call of Christ "Come, follow me and I will make you . . .".

> When the large church to which I belonged decided to plant a small church a couple of miles away, each member was asked to seek God's will for them, to stay at the church of 100 or so, or be a pioneer and part of something new. Twenty people felt called to plant the new church and so it began, with everyone having a part to play and gifts to use.

At 80 years old, Moses had a comfortable life as a shepherd, with a wife and family, but God called him from this comfortable life to something new and challenging. He spoke to Moses through a burning bush, outlining His plan to free the Israelites from the grip of the Egyptians. Then He dropped the bombshell telling Moses he was the man to lead them out! Moses in shock said "Who am I to go to Pharaoh?" God replied with these 5 words in Exodus 3v12 which should go with us everyday, "I will be with you", echoed in Matthew 28v20. Having God's presence with us through the Holy Spirit is enough. Whenever God asks us to do something, He equips us for the task. With increasing confidence, we can say: "I can do all things through Christ who strengthens me" (Phil 4v13 NIV).

A Paradigm Shift

What we believe is shown outwardly in our behaviour, and if we take on God's values, attitudes and character, it will speak volumes to the world about who we are and more importantly, who He is.

> Take on an entirely new way of life – a God fashioned life, a life renewed from the inside and working itself into your conduct as God accurately reproduces His character in you. (Ephesians 4v22 TM)

Some changes are made by God instantly when we meet Him for the first time, like the sailor who became a Christian and stopped swearing overnight. His shipmates noticed the difference straight away and asked what was going on as something had obviously happened to him. What an opportunity for the gospel.

Some changes in our thinking and living take longer, sometimes months or years. Learning to be like Jesus is a challenge because God's attitudes and values are often opposite to the way the world thinks. Christians are swimming against the tide in our society, but are often noticed in a positive way. Jesus works with us to realise our potential to be holy and constantly prays for us.

> So then, my brothers, because of God's great mercy to us I appeal to you: Offer yourselves as a living sacrifice to God, dedicated to his service and pleasing to him. This is the true worship that you should offer. Do not conform yourselves to the standards of this world, but let God transform you inwardly by a complete change of your mind. Then you will be able to know the will of God – what is good and is pleasing to him and is perfect. (Romans 12v1–2 TEV)

We need to look at ourselves and ask "If someone looks at my life as a Christian, what will they think God is like?" Our aim is to reflect the Son, Jesus Christ, to those around us and to be ambassadors in His name.

> Do all the good you can, by all the means you can, in all the ways you can, in all the places you can, at all the times you can, to all the people you can, as long as you ever can. (John Wesley)

Small Churches and New Disciples

When a person becomes a Christian, it is a very exciting moment especially for a small church. They may be the first convert for many years, or be the blessing following the hard work of reaching out to people locally. It is then easy to overwhelm them with courses and information, jobs and a list of "this is how we do things here". A small church though can be very effective in discipleship because the relationships potentially grow faster and people are happy to give time on a one-to-one basis.

New disciples need teaching on the basics of Christianity, starting from wherever they are on their spiritual journey and whatever their background, together with lots of gentle help. They have just had their lives turned upside down by Jesus Christ and that takes getting used to! Encouraging them to build a few relationships with mature Christians is helpful as they usually have many questions and want answers.

> When a small church recently found themselves with seven new Christians in one year, they were overwhelmed. Jesus had saved each of them from their sin and given them forgiveness, but they each learnt, experienced God and embraced their new life at different rates. As one size does not fit all, they each needed time to talk, unpack the past and explore this new life. This meant that other things were left undone and resources were stretched. It is a good problem to have, and the church got some things right and got some things wrong, hopefully learning from mistakes for next time.

We often refer to the church as a family, but care must be taken to explain what is meant to any new arrivals who may equate the word with abuse, violence, pain and loneliness. "Family" can also mean pressure and high expectations to some people. Having had it explained that family means love, support, acceptance and understanding, they may then conclude, wrongly, that in the church family there will never be a difference of opinion or conflict.

Knowing Your Gifts

> We are all parts of His one body, and each of us has different work to do. And since we are all one body in Christ, we belong to each other, and each of us needs all the others. God has given each of us the ability to do certain things well. (Romans 12v5–6 NLT)

In the church, each of us has different natural gifts and talents that God gave us at birth. All of these can be enhanced by the Holy Spirit to be used in God's service. We are uniquely designed and it is important for individuals to realise and acknowledge their own gifts and use them in service within the church. It is often easier to see gifts in others than yourself, so encouragement and affirmation is vital. God draws the people with the right gifts to accomplish His purpose in each church. Paul writes to the Ephesians saying:

> It was He who gave some to be apostles, some to be prophets, some to be evangelists, and some to be pastors and teachers, to prepare God's people for works of service, so that the body of Christ may be built up until we all reach unity in the faith and in the knowledge of the Son of God and become mature, attaining to the whole measure of the fullness of Christ. (Ephesians 4v11–13 NIV)

It could be said that each local church should have access to a clear leader, someone who hears God and acts on what he hears, someone who can enable others to witness to their faith, someone who is able to teach how to care and someone who is able to teach caringly. People on the whole do not like the pressure of being labelled but it is important to recognise and encourage their gifting.

There are many opportunities to serve God in any church, but in a small congregation, each person seems to be even more significant and their contribution can indeed be invaluable, whether making the tea, running a parent and toddler group, welcoming people or being prayer warriors. Each person of any age has a vital part to play, as Paul explained using the illustration of the church as a body in 1 Corinthians 12. All parts need to be functioning in harmony to enable the body to be healthy and move forward.

The small church is indeed a place where the whole is stronger than all the parts added together.

Growing In Our Faith

How do we experience growth in ourselves? It is often easier for others to see our progress, perhaps particularly so in a small church or homegroup setting where people know us well. We ourselves can feel progress is being made when we begin to consistently make decisions that are beneficial for us, and not damaging. Challenging negative habits or places we go to and turning them into positive habits and places is a sign of growth.

We should experience this growth as we get to know God better and trust Him more, so stay focused!

> Let your roots grow down into Christ and draw up nourishment from Him. See that you go on growing in the Lord, and become strong and vigorous in the truth. (Colossians 2v6–7 TLB)

God provides the resources we need for growth and it is important to make use of them, both as individuals and as (small) churches. Resources such as the Bible, study guides, prayer groups and brothers and sisters in the faith. As individuals grow in their faith, it affects the whole church and as churches grow spiritually so they increasingly affect the lives of those who attend and the people in the surrounding area.

The biggest and most risky prayer you can pray must be "Whatever, Lord". It encompasses "Whatever you want me to do, wherever you want me to go, and whenever you want me to." The aim of any disciple is to get to that point where we are willing in heart, soul and mind to pray this, having sacrificed our own agenda.

On The Journey

God calls us to join the adventure that is life outside our comfort zone, trusting Him no matter what. The journey will include times on the mountain top when God is so close, life is good and praise is on our lips all the time. We will also experience times on a plateau where we seem to do a lot of walking with no noticeable ups or downs. Those are times of learning to be with God in the everyday and enjoying His presence. Then comes the valleys, where life gets difficult with challenges, tough decisions, moral and ethical choices, when we are swayed by emotion, or when life throws all its unpleasantness at us. This is when we come to the end of ourselves and have to rely fully on God. He often gives us challenges that we haven't been through before so we can't just draw on experience, but have to step out in faith and rely on Him. At other times, he uses our life experiences to equip us for the next task. However, the valley is where fertile soil is found and it can be here that real but unseen growth takes place.

Small churches also experience these phases of the journey with times of blessing, new people, successful outreach events or answers to prayer. Then the "plateau" times of meeting together with quiet assurance and trust, but with no visitors over a number of months. There are also the valley times when the finances are low, people leave or there is illness, and it seems as though God is being very quiet. Those are often times of deepening fellowship and prayer, and when we need to hold onto the fact that God cares for His church, that He does have a plan and He is walking with us.

Bread For The Journey

God's word is living and builds us up as we feast on it daily. A challenging question for all disciples is "If you eat food like you read your Bible, how hungry would you be?"

Reading and memorising the words in the Bible is important as Moses wrote in Deuteronomy: "Fix these words of mine in your hearts and minds; tie them as symbols on your hands and bind them on your foreheads. Teach them to your children, talking about them when you sit at home and when you walk along the road, when you lie down and when you get up" (Deuteronomy 11v18–19 NIV).

The Holy Spirit can bring to mind only those things that we have already read and learnt. It is good to share thoughts and insights with other Christians at different stages on the journey in Bible study groups.

Power

Jesus promised power to his disciples, and this also means us today. "But you will receive power when the Holy Spirit comes on you; and you will be my witnesses in Jerusalem, and in all Judea and Samaria, and to the ends of the earth" (Acts 1v8 NIV).

Jesus knew that all disciples would need power to live and work for Him in this fallen world. Paul had experienced God's mighty power in his life in many ways (read Acts) and when he wrote to the church in Ephesus, who were living in a tough society as we do, he wanted them to know the full extent of God's power available to them through the name of Jesus. "I pray that out of his glorious riches he may strengthen you with power through his Spirit in your inner being, so that Christ may dwell in your hearts through faith" (Ephesians 3v16–17 NIV).

Consider how you and your church experience God's power. It is available for us now through the Holy Spirit and sets people on fire for Jesus. In a small church, we really need to experience God's power, not only to be refreshed and have the energy to keep going, but also to know and see His work among us, even though we may be few in number.

Wear Protective Gear

We have been provided with protection for the spiritual battles we shall face on this journey. Paul uses the uniform of a Roman soldier to illustrate the armour God has provided for us in Ephesians 6v13–18.

The Roman "tortoise" formation where 12 soldiers or more are standing shoulder to shoulder with their shields interlocking, preventing stones and arrows from inflicting damage is a good illustration for a small church. An up to date version of this illustration would be a small number of disciplined police forming a shield wall and being able to withstand a much larger force together. Even better if they are in a strategic place e.g. a small alley. Three of our main weapons in spiritual battles are Prayer, Praise and Personal Testimony, against which the devil cannot stand.

Prayer

Paul knew the power and effectiveness of prayer and wrote to the Ephesians:

> And pray in the Spirit on all occasions with all kinds of prayers and requests. With this in mind, be alert and always keep on praying for all the saints. Pray also for me, that whenever I open my mouth, words may be given me so that I will fearlessly make known the mystery of the gospel, for which I am an ambassador in chains. Pray that I may declare it fearlessly, as I should. (Ephesians 6v18–20 NIV)

It is good for disciples to meet together as a church, homegroup, prayer triplet etc. to pray and seek God together, to pray for each other and for those in need. While praying together in twos or threes builds confidence and helps develop relationships, we must also remember that "there is a world out there" in need of God's mercy and salvation (see Tools Section of Chapter 3).

Praying alone is vital because we all need those "God and me" times for growth in love and knowledge of Him. There are however times when prayer becomes difficult, especially when under spiritual attack, and it is at those times when we rely on others to pray for us. Give yourself a spiritual health check on a regular basis, as David did in Psalm 139: "Search me, O God, and know my heart; test me and know my anxious thoughts. See if there is any offensive way in me, and lead me in the way everlasting" (Psalm 139v23–24 NIV).

Praise

Power is released as we praise our Almighty God. The enemy cannot stand as God's name is exalted. In 2 Chronicles we read of invading armies being defeated as King Jehoshaphat followed God's instructions, put the musicians and singers at the head of the army and marched out singing loud praises to God.

> Early in the morning they left for the Desert of Tekoa. As they set out, Jehoshaphat stood and said, "Listen to me, Judah and people of Jerusalem! Have faith in the LORD your God and you will be upheld; have faith in his prophets and you will be successful."After consulting the people, Jehoshaphat appointed men to sing to the LORD and to praise him for the splendour of his holiness as they went out at the head of the army, saying: "Give thanks to the LORD, for his love endures for ever."
>
> As they began to sing and praise, the LORD set ambushes against the men of Ammon and Moab and Mount Seir who were invading Judah, and they were defeated. (2 Chronicles 20v20–22 NIV)

Personal Testimony

As a small church, we would like to see more people coming to Christ and joining us, and friendship evangelism is an effective way to grow the Kingdom. We each have a unique circle of contacts such as family, friends, workmates and neighbours who we can influence for God. Our daily lives following Jesus will impact on the people who know us best. As people watch how we live, speak and act, there are opportunities for us to tell them about Jesus. This task can be easier if we know what to say and are confident in saying it. See the Tools section at the end of the Chapter 4 for a framework for telling your story.

Serving An Audience Of One

> Be sure to fear the LORD and serve him faithfully with all your heart; consider what great things he has done for you. (1 Samuel 12v24 NIV)

Our call to salvation includes the call to service within the church. Wherever God calls us to be, in a church large or small, being in the service of the King is the best job to have, with all the resources of heaven available to us. We must at all times remember that we are serving an audience of One, the King of kings and the Lord of lords Himself.

There was once a concert pianist who, in front of a hushed, packed auditorium, played like he'd never played before. The music was exquisite and everyone was entranced. The wonderful music eventually came to an end and he bowed low. The audience applauded this young, gifted man and as he walked from the stage, they called for an encore. However, he refused to return and the stage manager tried to persuade him. The audience continued to clap and began to stand as they called again for an encore. The stage manager could not understand the pianist's reticence, telling him the audience were now on their feet. The pianist peeped at the auditorium through the curtain then turned sadly to the manager and said "I'm not playing an encore, because not *everyone* is standing." The stage manager looked again into the packed audience. "But everyone is standing apart from one old man." "Exactly" said the pianist. "That man is my teacher."

Our service is to the King alone, not looking for the applause of men. We serve the King by serving others, as graphically told by Jesus in the parable of the sheep and the goats in Matthew 25v34–40.

Aiming for excellence in all we do should be a code we live by and express in our service to Him, whether we clean the toilets or lead worship at the church. In our workplace, home, school gate or at the gym, we work and play for God, serving Him in the best way we can, with integrity, loyalty and fun. This includes keeping promises, being trustworthy, turning up on time, completing the task and not quitting.

Service is not optional. We are called to serve the King. In the Bible, God used all kinds of people with problems and excuses why they couldn't be used. However, He did use them, and usually in a mighty way. He can and will use you too.

Fix Your Eyes On Jesus

The writer to the Hebrews knew how life distracts us and after naming many heroes of our faith in chapter 11, goes on to encourage us to keep running our race in chapter 12, fixing our eyes on Jesus, with these heroes cheering us on from the stands. Jesus, our hero, kept going despite the cost of the cross, knowing He would get the prize (His bride) at the completion of the race. Paul wanted to complete the task Jesus had given him when he said: "However, I consider my life worth nothing to me, if only I may finish the race and complete the task the Lord Jesus has given me – the task of testifying to the gospel of God's grace" (Acts 20v24 NIV).

Each of us must give an account to God (Romans 14v12) of what we've done with our lives, if we followed Him or did our own thing. We alone are responsible for our relationship with God and our growth and we make choices every day to either live God's way or our way.

Nurturing Using Emmaus by Ruth Wood,
Gaer Baptist Church, Newport

I needed to provide nurture and possibly baptismal preparation for just one or two seekers at a time. These were church attenders in the 30–50 age group, who wanted to explore their faith further before making a decision about baptism. I chose the Emmaus course as it is very "open" in approach, encouraging lots of questions and presenting the gospel clearly without pushing any particular doctrinal stance. It can also be done as a 6 or 12 week course depending on the spiritual needs of the seekers. Weeks 7–12 cover discipleship issues such as prayer, Bible reading, fellowship, etc.

It worked well for us. There were two pairs of seekers in successive years, and each time one of the two went forward for baptism. Because the course was so informal, we were able to pause, take a break for work commitments, or spend an extra week on a difficult topic now and again. I would say Emmaus works best in a small group/housegroup setting (max. 4–5 people) but because of this, it is ideal for a small church where there are often only one or two seekers at time. However, the leader needs to be confident enough to present the material and work through the questions with people. There is no video/DVD presentation as far as I know.

Discipleship at Harlington Baptist Church by Bob Scott,
Harlington Baptist Church

The Alpha course has been run a number of times successfully at Harlington Baptist, with a meal first, a 45 minute video and then discussion. It has been a good foundational course for seekers, although it needed adapting.

We have recently found the new Alpha Express version of the course to be more suitable with a 30 minute video and a workbook for both leader and participants. This is better for those who are not "book people" and the Bible verses are on the screen during the video (Alpha is available in 60 languages).

Ongoing discipleship is made trickier because of our position as the nearest church to Heathrow Airport. Many people are transient, coming to the area to work for a short time, visiting or on shift work patterns. This makes continuity virtually impossible, so I write my own Bible Study notes and suit them to the people who come and the issues they face. We run a teaching series on Sunday mornings but have to recap the series on a regular basis for those who missed the week before.

DISCIPLESHIP TOOLS

Has the church got a plan for discipleship?

Example of a Discipleship Plan

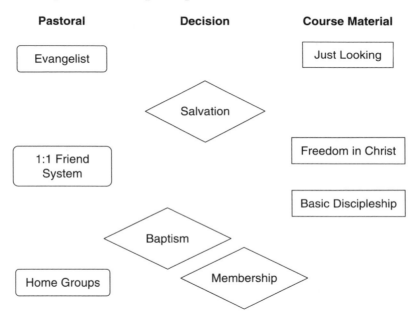

Pastoral	Decision	Course Material
Evangelist		Just Looking
	Salvation	
1:1 Friend System		Freedom in Christ
		Basic Discipleship
Home Groups	Baptism / Membership	

Key

Pastoral

Evangelist/Pastor – person speaking to seeker about Jesus and answering questions.

1:1 Friend System – Giving a new Christian a friend or "buddy" to talk to, pray with and generally be friends with is invaluable.

Home Groups – Integration into home based groups for Bible study and fellowship can happen at any time on this journey.

Decision

Salvation – When a person commits (or recommits) their life to Christ.

Baptism – When a Christian makes a public declaration of an inward decision by going into the water (dying to self) and out of the water (raising to new life in Christ).

Membership – An understanding of responsibilities held by members of the local church, a decision to join and a decision by the church to welcome them.

Course Material[1]

"Just Looking" courses – Once people are interested in knowing more about the gospel, inviting them to a short course is helpful e.g. Emmaus, Alpha, Christianity Explored, Y Course.

The Freedom in Christ course – Experience shows that most people have issues, especially lack of forgiveness, which they bring into their new life. This course among others helps them to discover who they are now in Christ and how to leave the past behind.

Basic teaching about Christianity courses – Basic teaching which covers foundations of faith, including baptism and communion e.g. Life Course from CPO, Purpose Driven Life.

Make sure you adapt the teaching to the ability of the person being taught eg. non book people, non readers, people with learning difficulties, visually impaired etc.

Be prepared to spend time teaching on a one-to-one basis rather than wait for enough people for a group.

From here, the new disciple must be encouraged not only to learn from the preaching, study in a small group and to learn privately, but also to bring their many non-Christian friends along to discover Christ for themselves.

---

[1] There are a number of resources mentioned here, see Chapter 9 for details.

Questions About New Disciples

These questions and suggested answers are designed for Leaders.

What are your thoughts about a one-to-one or "buddy system"?
New Christians may have very different issues / background / ages to the majority of members. Culture and class issues can bring some interesting reactions to 'normal' church life. Some of the background history of the new people can be very disturbing, but only known to a few in confidence. A one-to-one friendship, prayer and support system works well but needs commitment on both sides. Early integration into the small groups may be helpful, if the church has them.

What might need to change to cater for the new disciples' needs?
Consider as a small church how you might need to change to cater for the newcomers needs. Why should "they" always be the ones to fit in with "us"? Do we teach them at a level they can understand? Do you give them appropriate levels of responsibility at an appropriate time? (Take into account what they do at work.)

Is the church welcoming (or not) or over-powering to new Christians?
Current members/older Christians who have been committed to life in a small church, are probably very regular attendees and generally have a "we'll muck in" philosophy. We must not necessarily expect the same approach from new Christians, putting unnecessary pressure on them. In today's culture, attending anything once or twice a month counts as "regular attendance". There is also the possibility that new people arriving into a close-knit community may be seen as a threat.

Does the church appreciate the time it takes for people to adjust to their new life in Jesus?
Watch out that the new believer's early enthusiasm isn't abused by the church's desperate need for workers – limit any responsibilities

taken on in the first few months. A newly converted primary school teacher might look like God's gift to the Sunday school, but they may really appreciate a rest or serving in other ways in the church.

How does the church cope when new people leave?
As lives change, people feel more able to re-integrate into society. For example, a person whose life is in a mess comes to Christ. The church helps to build them up, they are now able to hold down a job and become too busy or "don't need church any more". At this point they sometimes withdraw from church. This transition needs to be recognised and the regular one-to-one contact for friendship, support and prayer set up when they first arrive will help to keep them in touch. If people leave, it is always important to part on friendly non-critical terms, leaving the door open for return. Sometimes people who leave keep in contact with some individuals (often their buddy) and subsequently, when they call for help when in trouble, find that the church is still there for them.

Questions about Discipleship

This list of questions is designed for the Church Leadership to review and discuss with the small group teachers.

- Are there opportunities for learning together in groups?
- How are people encouraged to develop their gifts and talents?
- Is there a teaching plan running through the year in the groups?
- Is there a preaching plan running through the year?
- Is the Gospel told regularly in public services?
- How are people encouraged in their daily lives to follow Jesus?
- Is the Bible central in your church? Is it accepted as God's truth?
- Do you experience God's touch as you meet together to praise Him?

- Is there time for the Holy Spirit to speak or act through people as you meet together?
- Is there a church prayer meeting? Is it well attended?
- Do you have intercessors in the church?
- Are prayer partners or triplets set up?
- Are people confident about telling others about Jesus?
- Do you practice telling testimonies/stories to each other? (What God did in your life last week is as powerful as when you first came to know Him).
- How do you encourage people to serve both inside and outside the church?

Worksheet

In a small group, share with each other the *prayer* life and ministry of your church, and how it could be enhanced.

What new things could you be doing in your church if more people were *committed* to Kingdom ministry?

How do you *encourage* people in your church to become more involved?

Apart from Sunday worship, what other ways do people in your church have opportunity to receive the *Word of God*?

Bible Study

Encouraging each other is an important part of discipleship. This is a study from 2 Corinthians to help you to "keep on keeping on".

1. 2 Corinthians 8v12 – The gift is acceptable according to what you have, not what you don't have. God accepts, delights in and appreciates what we try to do for Him and He does not condemn our church for being small and somewhat limited. An Alpha course with just one participant, run by a church with 6 members, is as much a joy to God's heart as one with 30 guests run by a 200

member church. Give the gift, service, effort or prayer time. Give, use, invest what you have and don't worry about what you don't have.

2. 2 Corinthians 9v6 – Sowing generously means reaping generously. No effort we ever make to reach out to others is ever wasted. Remember the sower in the parable? 75% of what he sowed came to nothing, but the 25% that grew yielded a hundred times more than was sown. More than enough to make up for all the seed that didn't survive. Sow generously and use the little you have willingly and often – not just one attempt to leaflet the houses but half a dozen – not just one outreach service but several a year – not just one non-Christian friendship nurtured but a whole circle of them . . . and the harvest will come.

3. 2 Corinthians 9v8 – God is able. You may feel helpless and under-resourced, but God can provide all that you need so you abound in every good work. No church leader can ever say "I have got very little to work with." Isn't God enough for you? So learn to say "We have two members still able-bodied, six over 85 and God. What shall we do to reach out?

4. 2 Corinthians 9v10 – We are protected from burnout. Two things are provided here, seed to sow and bread for food. The two biggest needs of a small church leadership team are enough gifts and abilities and opportunities to do what needs to be done (the seed to grow) and enough strength and stamina to keep doing it (bread for food). God provides both.

God accepts and appreciates our service. He is able and works with us and He provides what we need to do the work and keep going ourselves. Be encouraged!

Internal Church Survey

This exercise is very useful in discovering gifts and talents in your church, so ideally each member should take part.

1. Know who you are in Christ – accepted by Him as you are, special to Him (He loves you!) and able to trust Him for today and the future. Read Ephesians Chapter 1.

2. Look back on life's experiences; see how they have formed you and how you can use them to help others. Write them in a notebook. We can empathise and come alongside people more effectively if we have had a similar experience, but we must deal with any emotional damage of our own hurts before helping others.

3. Ask yourself "what would I love to do for God? What would I love to see happen in our church? What are my passions, hopes and dreams?" Write your answers in your notebook then talk about them with your leaders and pray together.

4. Look at the talents and gifts God gave you at birth and see if they are being used in service for Him. We all love doing things that we are good at and God gave us these abilities for a reason. We function best as a "round peg in a round hole." It is also good to know what you are not good at. Write these down in your notebook.

5. What kind of personality are you? – Introvert or extrovert, loud or quiet, talkative or reserved. Write this down too. Although God can increase our confidence in Him, He uses who we are in service for him.

6. God equips us spiritually at our re-birth and knowing what our gifts are and how to use them is essential. What do you do regularly that you know is God working out through you? Write these down in the notebook, then look up the following scriptures:

1 Corinthians 12v4–11
Romans 12v6–16
Ephesians 4v11–13

You are a unique creation by God, so try not to compare yourself with anyone else, or be restricted in your service by the expectation of others.

All of these reflections are often easier if talked through with a mature Christian who has known you for some time. It is usually more obvious to an observer what our gifts are, than to ourselves. Take your notebook with you to reflect on what you have written, during the conversation. If everyone in your church does this exercise (often referred to as a skills audit) then the spread of gifts and talents will be known. It is important that each one plays an active role using their gifts to fulfil the corporate vision.

Have A Go!

One way to find out what church members are capable of without committing the church to something it can't sustain, is to try one-off events first:

- A children's fun evening for an age group you feel comfortable with.
- A single coffee morning or lunch for the elderly.

These "trial runs" help to build confidence and learn from mistakes, perhaps discovering unrecognised gifts and finding out what church members enjoy doing, without scaring yourselves to death!

CHAPTER THREE

BEING GOD'S PEOPLE

"If many small people do many small things in many small places, we can change the face of the earth." (On screen at the Baptist Assembly 2006)

The Church is God's Plan A to reach a needy world. There is no Plan B.

Christ is the head of the church and we must always keep Him in that position. It's His church, His money and His work that we do.

In chapter one of his letter to the Church in Colossae, Paul tells about Jesus and His relationship with them, reminding them: "And he is the head of the body, the church; he is the beginning and the firstborn from among the dead, so that in everything he might have the supremacy" (Colossians 1v18 NIV).

A church is a group of any number of those who believe in God the Father, Son and Holy Spirit, and is described in the Bible as a body (1 Colossians 1v18), a household (Ephesians 2v19) and a bride (Revelation 19v7–8). They are people who have repented, committed their lives to God and are serving Him together. They usually meet in a building, (sometimes in the open air), and readily welcome people from all walks of life to join them in services and social events.

God's top priority for us is that we are spiritual people empowered by Him, as Paul wrote to the Ephesians: "[God's] intent was that now, through the church, the manifold wisdom of God should be made known to the rulers and authorities in the heavenly realms, according to his eternal purpose, which he accomplished in Christ Jesus our Lord" (Ephesians 3v10–11 NIV).

The people of God globally are the bride of Christ described in Revelation 21v2–3 and we will live forever in an international community worshipping our sovereign God. We have an opportunity to demonstrate this unity now on earth being God's own people. In the New Testament, there are more than thirty "one another" instructions written to the church about how to get along with people of all colours, cultures and backgrounds. These commands make a good series to study and work on in a practical way. As we come to Christ, we often bring worldly attitudes that need to be changed to be more like the attitudes of Jesus.

Meanwhile, we rub along together having to learn the basics about putting each other first, how to function as a family of God and not being judgmental. A small church is often a good context for learning to keep our feet firmly on the ground even while reaching for heavenly things.

The time came for our student pastor to do his obligatory "taped service"; a key part of his course. We were all on our best behaviour, determined to sing the songs well, and listen attentively during the sermon. The oldest of our small band of 20 adjusted his hearing aid. The tape recorder was switched on and the service commenced. We worshipped and prayed and read Scripture; then the student started his sermon. Cajoling, remonstrating, teaching, encouraging; he gave his all. Reaching the climax, he took a dramatic silent pause. At that key point, the oldest person's chin wavered and an almighty snore broke forth from his mouth! The meeting deteriorated into laughter and the student had to resort to a re-run the following week.

Be an Inclusive Church

His name is Bill. He has wild hair, wears a T-shirt with holes in it, jeans and no shoes. This was literally his wardrobe for his entire 4 years at college. He is brilliant. Kind of esoteric and became a Christian while attending college. Across the street from the campus is a well-dressed, very conservative church. They want to develop a ministry to the students but are not sure how to go about it.

One day, Bill decides to go there. He walks in with no shoes, jeans, his T-shirt and wild hair. The service has already started and so Bill starts down the aisle looking for a seat. The church is completely packed and he can't find a seat. By now, people are looking a bit uncomfortable, but no one says anything. Bill gets closer and closer to the pulpit and when he realises there are no seats; he just squats down right there on the carpet. (Although perfectly acceptable behaviour at a college fellowship, this had never happened at this church before!) By now the people are really uptight and the tension in the air is thick.

About this time, the minister realises that from the back of the church a deacon is slowly making his way toward Bill. Now the deacon is in his eighties, has silver grey hair and a three-piece suit. A godly man, very elegant, very dignified and very courtly. He walks with a cane and, as he starts walking towards this boy, everyone is saying to themselves that

A TOOLBOX FOR SMALL CHURCHES

you can't blame him for what he's going to do. How can you expect a man of his age and his background to understand some college kid on the floor? It takes a long time for the man to reach the boy. The church is utterly silent except for the clicking of the man's cane. All eyes are focused on him. You can't even hear anyone breathing.

The minister can't even preach the sermon until the deacon does what he has to do. And now they see the elderly man drop his cane to the floor. With great difficulty, he lowers himself and sits down next to Bill and worships with him so he won't be alone. Everyone chokes up with emotion.

When the minister gains control, he says "What I'm about to preach, you will never remember. What you have just seen, you will never forget. Be careful how you live. You may be the only Bible some people will ever read."[1]

Is Everyone Welcome To Your Church?

Male or Female	Alcoholic	Disabled
Straight or Gay	Single Parent	High Flyer
Drug Addict	Older Person	Rich or Poor
Baby/Child	Teenager	Unemployed
Abused	Ex-Prisoner	Foreigner
Black or White	Asylum Seeker	Married or Partnered

This list is endless.

Here there is no Greek or Jew, circumcised or uncircumcised, barbarian, Scythian, slave or free, but Christ is all, and is in all. Therefore, as God's chosen people, holy and dearly loved, clothe yourselves with compassion, kindness, humility, gentleness and patience. (Colossians 3v11–12 NIV)

A small church has to be open-hearted, warm and welcoming to all. If it is not perceived as such, then it dies. In a small church there is no room to hide. It is not possible to disguise prejudice or intolerance from those who know you well. Visitors know if the welcome is genuine or not and react accordingly.

---

[1] Thanks to Sam Tolbert, Tranquil United Methodist Church, Greenwood, S. Carolina, USA.

Belonging, Believing, Behaving

> A small church is ideal for fellowship; you can worship in a large crowd but true fellowship requires a small group.

Belonging

Belonging is a major part of being in a community and people feel that they belong when they are valued and have a purpose. To grow, a plant has to put down roots, and people too need that sense of belonging and stability to enable growth. A small church can provide that sense of belonging as relationships are built. The advantage is that relationships can be built with the whole church and newcomers can feel they have influence and value.

Believing

When people feel welcomed for who they are, trust will be built and they will be more likely to listen to what we believe. It is helpful to have a written "Statement of Faith" to give to enquirers. It is good to encourage the church to talk about their faith and about what they believe and why. In a small church it is less of an ordeal for someone to stand up and share what they believe.

Behaving

People always behave according to what they believe but, as their beliefs change, the behaviour changes as people take Jesus teaching to heart. We must be aware that in society there is a perceived code of "how to behave in church" and many people outside the church feel they won't live up to it.

> A lady once said "I'm not good enough to come to church", not realising that we would welcome her for who she was, not for how she behaved.

New Christians take time to adjust to their new life and we need to be sensitive to this. The expectations must be real and we must help them to belong, then believe, then behave. Often we get this order wrong and expect too much too soon, like assuming knowledge where there is none.

Paul writes to a variety of new churches in the New Testament about how to behave as the people of God. They were getting it wrong and needed correction, so do we.

> Therefore, as God's chosen people, holy and dearly loved, clothe your-selves with compassion, kindness, humility, gentleness and patience. Bear with each other and forgive whatever grievances you may have against one another. Forgive as the Lord forgave you. And over all these virtues put on love, which binds them all together in perfect unity. Let the peace of Christ rule in your hearts, since as members of one body you were called to peace. And be thankful. (Colossians 3v12–15)

The church needs to be a place where people can be invited, wel-comed and experience God. If we are not comfortable inviting our friends to church or an event, we need to be asking why and addressing the issue. We may feel that by inviting our friends to our small church may lead to them being overwhelmed with the "friendly" questions that may be asked or that they will be obvi-ously new and attract much attention. We just may be embarrassed that there are so few people there.

Membership

"The whole is greater than the sum of its parts"

As Jesus calls us into His global family, it is essential for our growth and development to be a part of a local church family. He talks of church in terms of "the flock" and "branches of the vine" in the gospels (see John chapters 10 and 15) and calls twelve men into fellowship to follow Him together. In Acts 2 we see how the church met together often in small groups to learn, share, break bread and pray. We get a strong sense of belonging as we read these verses. Each person is gifted by God in different ways and in a small church especially, it is vital that people share the roles and responsibilities, using their natural talents and spiritual gifts.

In Baptist churches, membership is significant as it brings responsibilities to those who have decided to commit themselves to the local body of Christ. The "how people become members" varies considerably across the churches, but the commitment required is the same. Some people find it difficult to commit to a church for an unspecified period of time due to circumstances, so a way forward may be to ask the people to commit themselves as members of the church for a year. Because this has an end date, it feels possible and energy, time and money can be put into something achievable rather than a "signing up for life" arrangement. This may be the practical way ahead especially for churches in the big cities where life is so transient. It could also challenge people from larger churches to commit to a small church for a year.

Decisions about all aspects of church life are made at church meetings, hopefully through praying and seeking God's will together. Small churches are usually more concerned about people than activity, but decisions about mission and fabric have to be made. Care must be taken to stay focussed on God, especially if the discussion is getting heated or if there are strong personalities dominating the debate.

Unity is vital and Jesus took time in the Garden of Gethsemane to pray for unity between believers (see John 17v23).

Together Making Jesus Known

Reaching out to a needy world is part of our purpose as Jesus himself said:

> "The Spirit of the Lord is on me, because he has anointed me to preach good news to the poor. He has sent me to proclaim freedom for the

prisoners and recovery of sight for the blind, to release the oppressed, to proclaim the year of the Lord's favour." (Luke 4v18–19 NIV)

Working together to extend the Kingdom with one heart and purpose in a Christ-centered church is what we all wish to be a part of. Prayer is vital and listening to both the written and revealed word of God is essential. Knowing God's word and being able to share it with others is an important part of church life, as well as having a heart for the community (see "How to Share your Faith" in the Tools section in Chapter 4).

The church is often seen as a hospital to which broken people come to find healing, with the minister being a kind of GP, knowing a bit about everything. The leader's role could be more like that of a hospital manager, overseeing and co-ordinating an efficient team of specialists (A minister could also be likened to an orchestra conductor bringing people in, involving their unique contribution at the right time and so together producing something beautiful). Ideally a church should be a place for people come to for help from God and people, and find Jesus to be the answer.

Paul writes:

Now finish the work, so that your eager willingness to do it may be matched by your completion of it, according to your means. For if the willingness is there, the gift is acceptable according to what one has, not according to what he does not have. (2 Corinthians 8v11–12 NIV)

Closure

When things seem to be hopeless and circumstances are working against you, the building is costing more money to upkeep than is available, only a few people are left who cannot carry on or that the job you were called to do has been completed, it is important to stop and ask God "Should we close?" This is a very brave prayer but it focuses prayer meetings like nothing else I have known! We have had to face this question twice in our church's short history of 24 years, when humanly speaking, the odds were against us.

The first time came after we had enabled two people to train as Baptist Ministers, but who were then called to pastor elsewhere. We applied for a full-time minister to work with us, but despite a number of candidates, it came to nothing. What was God saying? Do we carry on? How? God answered our prayers by calling a church member to leave his senior post in industry to be our new pastor.

The second time we asked this question followed an eviction notice from the Church of England who wanted to sell their building we borrowed on a Sunday to a developer. We explored a number of possibilities such as using another building, merging with a local church or closing. We were again at a crossroads. After much soul searching, angst and prayer, God stepped in by providing us with new premises of a youth centre that was not only a better building, but cheaper! It is good for a church to get to their knees over this issue. If God says it is time to close, then carrying on is futile. If God says to continue His work, it gives new focus, purpose and energy to the congregation. At the time of writing, we have just been told that the County Council want to close the Youth Centre where we meet. We may have to ask the "Should we close" question again and see what God says.

There are other options to explore before closure such as moving out of a crumbling building and renting a local venue, or amalgamating with another church (see Chapter 7 for stories of amalgamation and resurrection). It is good to consult your Regional Team when considering any of these options.

More information on Church Closures in the Baptist Union Guidelines at www.baptist.org.uk or phone 01235 517700 for a paper copy.

Believing God against the Odds by Fiona Weatherhead, Secretary of Hampton Baptist Church, Middlesex

"What is a small church like Hampton Baptist Church (about 30 members) going to do with a full-time minister as well as a minister in training?" you may ask. But at a special church meeting held on Sunday 25th July 2006, the members voted unanimously to call Steve Jenkins as our Minister-in-Training.

So, how did this call come about? We knew that Steve was being called to the ministry, as, at a church meeting on the 11th October 2005, we voted unanimously that Steve, along with his wife Debbie be recommended for the ministry. On the 14th December last year Steve went before the Ministerial Recognition Committee for Baptist Ministry and was accepted. This was closely followed in February by him being accepted into Spurgeon's College and at this point Steve began to look for a student placement.

On the 31st March the church held a half night of prayer at the chapel. At the end of the meeting both Paul Hill, one of our elders, and Tim, our pastor, looked up and the two of them felt that God was saying that Steve should be called to Hampton Baptist Church. Both Paul and Tim felt a strong sense of God's calling and they discussed this with Debbie, Steve's wife, as she was at that prayer meeting. However, they couldn't see how this was possible. We are already on Home Mission, which means that we get a grant from the Baptist Union to help pay for Tim's stipend. So how could we possibly afford the extra salary and expenses of a minister in training?

On the 5th April, 5 days after the prayer meeting, the leadership minutes record the following:

Thought Steve was called to work as a student pastor in HBC. Barbara (the Treasurer) felt it was early days yet and that many churches don't make a decision about student pastorships until June; that Steve and Debbie are definitely in her view called to the Baptist ministry, but need to be willing to go wherever God sends them; that it might not be easy to obtain approval for this at a church meeting; and that availability of the funding could be a "fleece" to determine whether we considered the matter further.

By the next leaders meeting in May the funding had become available. A person, or persons, unknown had pledged to cover the housing allowance and wages for Steve for the whole three-year course. God had honoured our fleece.

In June we took this information to the church meeting, and asked people to pray about the situation and in July our treasurer outlined the full extent of our commitment to this proposal and the financial implications.

We then gave people time to think this over and pray – which takes me back to that Special Church Meeting in July when Steve was eventually called to serve HBC as a Minister-in-Training.

So, where do we go from here? We now have Tim and Steve, 29 members and a building that isn't literally falling down, but which does require significant expenditure if it is going to remain in an upright position. We're seeking after God's heart now, and asking him for a new vision – where do we serve, do we stay in the current location or do we move somewhere else, where should we be putting our energies? We are excited and yet challenged, we have received warnings and positive pictures, we want to go in the right direction, in God's direction.

"My thoughts are nothing like your thoughts," says the Lord. "And my ways are far beyond anything you could imagine. For just as the heavens are higher than the earth, so my ways are higher than your ways and my thoughts higher than your thoughts". (Isaiah 55v8–9 from the NLT)

Coming to a Campus Near You . . . by David Sutcliffe, Sutton Bonington Baptist Church, Leicestershire

Sutton Bonington is a small village just 10 miles south of Nottingham and the start of the autumn term is the reason for a significant increase in the population of eighteen to twenty some-things. Students from across the UK and from many different parts of the world converge on the Sutton Bonington campus of the University of Nottingham. The village has a population of about 1300 but is boosted by about 50% when the university students arrive.

So what does this mean for a small village church? The Baptist Church in Sutton Bonington has a membership of about 40, but swells significantly at our Sunday services, as each autumn there are new additions to the congregation from the campus. Some are UK undergraduates straight from school, others come for post-graduate studies from Africa, India, Asia and Continental Europe with varied denominational and cultural backgrounds. Many of these overseas visitors have made great sacrifices to come and study – some bring their families but others leave young children in the care of the extended family at home. They often have to exercise a very practical faith for the everyday necessities of life in the high cost economy to which they have come. It is a privilege for us, as a small local church, to offer friendship, hospitality and practical help to those who initially find our ways and customs so different from their own. Many Christian international students are hungry for fellowship and we hold a weekly evening Bible study meeting in a home as well as a regular daytime opportunity for wives of some of the students to get together.

The most rewarding aspect of this work is to see spiritual growth in faith and understanding in many of these international visitors. They come to study in an intellectual "centre of excellence" but by the grace of God they find much more than academic qualifications alone.

One of the most remarkable aspects of this global mobility is the opportunity to get to know visiting students from countries where the Christian gospel cannot be freely proclaimed. Their studies in the UK have given many visiting friends the opportunity to hear about Jesus for the first time so in our weekly internationals Bible study we have a separate group for the "not-yet Christians".

Student mobility is one of the Lord's creative ways of ensuring that the good news continues to be heard! What a privilege to welcome visitors from all nations.

Some years ago, it became clear that God was giving us opportunities to minister to overseas visitors, but we needed some specific resources. The Lord opened up the opportunity for us to work with Friends International, an organisation which exists to encourage UK churches to minister to visiting international students. We now have a part-time Friends International worker on the campus as part of the University chaplaincy and she is a vital link between Christians in the village and the student community.

As a church we are privileged to be able to support the University's Christian Union in prayer and the students enrich our music group and some help with our youth groups. In recent years it has been exciting to see a significant growth in the CU both in terms of numbers and in the desire to share Jesus on our local campus. This has followed a period when the CU was much smaller and less active. So the appropriate support from the church has to reflect the changing needs and opportunities of our student friends.

Strains and stresses? Diversity and variety can lead to some issues regarding styles of worship or particular emphases but it's a great preparation for heaven! There are sometimes particular issues of pastoral care for those who may be struggling with being far from home and family. However, the greatest drawback to having a student congregation is the frequent farewells to those who have become good friends and "family" during their stay.

In Sutton Bonington, we thank God for the joy of sharing in the lives of these young people and, in some small measure, helping them to grow in the grace and knowledge of the Lord Jesus Christ.

BEING GOD'S PEOPLE TOOLS

How do you measure Success in a Small Church?
Growing contacts with people outside the church? Number of baptisms? Consider the level of participation and involvement of people and the commitment of members to attend church meetings or house groups and personal breakthroughs that have built faith. Success is about changed lives and growth, bridges built or hurting people touched by the love of Jesus

Questions For Small Group Discussion

General

- What are the advantages of being a small church?
- What attracts people to it?
- What does it accomplish *because* it is small?
- What would you miss if it doubled in size?
- What do you think small churches can teach larger ones?
- What are the drawbacks in being a small church?
- What would you most like to change about your church?

People Connections

- Look at the community around the church – does the church have the same mix of people?
- Look at people groups – what is the ethnic mix and age spread?
- Do we aim to be a local church for local people or a network church which grows through personal friendships? Or both?

Welcome, Inclusion

- Getting people over the threshold into the church building for the first time is a challenge.
- Does the church building look inviting from the outside?

- Are the notice boards up to date and attractive? Are they in the "local languages"?
- Is there a welcome at the door?
- Is *everyone* welcome regardless of class, culture, race, sexual orientation, dress or age?
- What do people see as they walk in?
- What is the response when a person arrives late?
- What is the atmosphere like on a Sunday in church? Friendly or cold?
- Can visitors sit anywhere they choose? Is "who sits where" an issue?
- Are visitors spoken to after the service or do church people just talk to each other?
- Is there information available about the church for visitors to take home? Is it in a variety of languages?

Belonging

- How do you make people feel that they belong?
- Do you know the mix of gifts and talents there are in the church?
- How can you best use them to present the gospel?
- Is the church accepting of new people with new ideas?

Believing

- Is it clear what the church believes? Have you a Statement of Faith?
- Is the gospel presented regularly in a way that is easy to understand?
- Are there opportunities for people to ask questions and discuss Bible texts?
- Are there opportunities for people to make a decision for Christ?
- Are people encouraged to consider baptism early in their Christian lives?

Behaving

- Are people accepted regardless of their behaviour? Safety must be taken into consideration, but do people feel free to be themselves?

- Do we love people enough to see the person they are and their potential despite their outward behaviour?

Membership

- How do you encourage commitment: To God? To the church family? To making Jesus known in the area?
- Reflect on the process by which people become members in your church. Is it the most welcoming approach or should there be changes?
- Is there much difference between members and non-members in your church?
- Do the members live locally? Are they part of the community or do they commute?
- Do people work together as a team? Are they happy to serve, no matter what the task?
- Is giving a priority? Money, time, effort, possessions, people . . .
- How well do the people in church know each other?
- Do they just meet on Sundays or at meetings?
- Do you have socials where people can have fun together?
- Are single people befriended by families or is there a singles group?
- Do children feel included or excluded from the church family?
- If people have issues with commitment, consider using a one-year covenant scheme instead of or as well as ordinary membership. It enables people to be more short term about their commitment. They are less likely to have issues signing up for 1 year than they are if they have a perception of membership as a life sentence.

Making Jesus Known

Are we ready as a church to free the prisoners, help the blind to see and to release the oppressed through God's power? How might we do this in our local area?

Have we a heart for the poor and hurting, the rejects of society, including those who reject their own worth? How can come we alongside and encourage people?

Be a Praying Church – Reflection

Personal prayer – It is important to pray for yourself by yourself, but asking for prayer from others and praying for others is part of what church is. There may be opportunity during intercessory prayers in a service, or asking someone privately to pray for you. It is important to go and pray with someone if you feel prompted by God. This is usually welcomed, especially in a small church because of the nature of the relationship already built. It is good to encourage intercessors (people who love to pray intensely and fervently for others on a regular basis) as they have a very powerful ministry.

Prayer partners and triplets – People meeting to pray together on a weekly basis to share personal issues in prayer as well as outside concerns.

Prayer Chain – a list of the church members where the first person on the list is told the prayer need, that one contacts the next on the list and so on. In these days of technology, prayer needs can quickly be made known via email or text messages.

Prayer Meeting – This should be the power house of the church and not boring! It is an opportunity to gather as church to celebrate who God is and to seek Him. It is helpful when meeting together to pray aloud, so all present can say "Amen" to the prayers. Pictures, words or scriptures can be brought and shared in an attitude of prayer. It is good to keep a record of prayers, words or visions for future reference and they can be crossed out as prayers are answered and God is glorified.

Prayer Walking – Prayer walking the area around the church ("the parish") is a powerful tool. As you bring the area to God in prayer, He speaks through things you see and feel as well as giving you opportunities to talk to people. Pray for peace in the homes, prosperity for the area and hearts softened towards the gospel. We regularly drive through familiar streets, yet we get a totally different perspective on foot. Each member (or pair) could be allocated a road to pray for and deliver invitations to so that the whole community is covered in prayer.

Extended times of Prayer – this can be several hours, half a night, all day or all night set aside to seek God when a big decision needs to be made or a major crisis is looming. This requires a sacrifice of time and energy, but time spent with God and each other is never disappointing.

Prayer Questions

- Do people consider prayer as a priority?
- Are there prayer partners or triplets in our church?
- Is there a prayer chain set up for those urgent situations that need support?
- Is there a time when the church can come together to pray?
- Is there an area or "parish" that we are seeking to reach, where prayer walking could be effective? Walking or cycling is better than driving. Designating each local road to a church member or prayer partnership regularly covers the area in prayer.
- Do we have extended times of prayer, either for big issues, or just spending time before God together?

S.W.O.T. Analysis

An effective tool used by both secular management and churches for gaining a perspective of the situation in order to develop the way forward (see Appendix for a biblical background to S.W.O.T.). This exercise requires a high percentage of the committed people to be involved, a high degree of honesty and very specific, not general answers. This exercise is often more effective if facilitated by a person from outside the church (contact your local area team)

On each of 4 large sheets of paper, write these headings:

Strengths
Weaknesses
Opportunities
Threats

Under the headings, write down the things the church are good at, the weaknesses to address, the specific opportunities on the doorstep or in the short-term future, and what threatens the work going ahead.

When the 4 sheets have between 5 and 10 items listed under each heading, prioritise the top 3 that need working on and discuss the way forward together.

Small Group Activity

"Do the same things but better"

Choose one area of your church life as it is now e.g. worship, midweek meeting, newsletter, welcome, pastoral care.

Share ideas in small groups of how it could be better.

Discuss how you could make changes with the resources and people you already have.

CHAPTER FOUR

MISSION, GROWTH AND CHANGE

"Jesus turned the world upside down with only 12 people, so I don't see why it shouldn't work in Cricklewood!"

Why Mission?

Because God is a missionary God, God's people are missionary people. The church's mission is not secondary to its being, the church exists in being sent and in building up itself for its mission. Karl Barth, Theologian

The church has often been described as the only club on earth that exists for the benefit of its non-members. This is just as true for a small church. The purpose of the church is to fulfil the Great Commission:

> Then Jesus came to them and said, "All authority in heaven and on earth has been given to me. Therefore go and make disciples of all nations, baptising them in the name of the Father and of the Son and of the Holy Spirit, and teaching them to obey everything I have commanded you. And surely I am with you always, to the very end of the age." (Matthew 28v18–20 NIV)

Quite simply, God wants all men to be saved: "The Lord is not slow in keeping his promise, as some understand slowness. He is patient with you, not wanting anyone to perish, but everyone to come to repentance" (2 Peter 3v9 NIV).

It is an essential part of our call to communicate to the world the presence of God, His power at work in us and in creation, and to bring His word to people.

Our mission is to extend the Kingdom of God, making Jesus known through the power of the Holy Spirit, by bringing people within earshot of the call of Christ. It is not optional.

About 15 years ago, there was a small church whose leadership team, while reviewing the church activities, realised that although they were growing together well and worshipping God, the mission aspect was lacking. With no leaders gifted in evangelism to lead the way, they decided to get outside help in the shape of a student from Spurgeon's College, studying evangelism and church planting. The church agreed and a few months later, the student arrived. At first, some of his new ideas seemed scary e.g. knocking on doors to give out gospels, but as the church began to step out of their comfort zone, God honoured their efforts and their fear subsided. After 4 years of establishing regular open-air events, meals with a meaning, Just Looking Courses and barbecues in the park for the locals, the student qualified and felt called to minister elsewhere. But the mission mindset had been established and carried on. As new people arrived, they were happy to be part of a church that was outward looking and community minded. Thanks to the humility of those leaders, mission has been placed high on the church agenda ever since.

How do we reach out with the Gospel?

Every person is either a missionary or a mission field.

Mission can be as simple or as complex as we want to make it. The gospel in its simplest form is: "For God so loved the world that he gave his one and only Son, that whoever believes in him shall not perish but have eternal life" (John 3v16 NIV).

Personal Mission

The important thing is that mission is seen as a priority and always on the agenda, personally as well as corporately. Each of us is unique and has a personal connection with a group of people that no one else has: our spouse, parents, brothers & sisters, children, relations, neighbours, colleagues and friends. We need to see this as our personal mission field.

When Amanda recommitted her life to God recently, she wanted to share her story with her neighbours, so they too might know her joy. She wrote her testimony on a small card, added the phone number of our church, and posted it through doors in her street. As a result of this, the church now has contact with 5 homes and 5 people committed their lives to Christ. She then brought along another friend to a church event, who also gave her life to Jesus! This is personal mission in action.

Mission should naturally flow from each of us (we are all mission-aries) as we live our life in the world, as we have opportunities to talk to people about our faith, bringing hope for the future.

Mission Together

> "The church exists by mission as a fire exists by burning."
> Emil Brunner

Mission is crucial for small churches, because if no new people are coming to Christ and joining us, the church will shrink and eventually die. In a large church there are more people around to do mission off their own bat, or to flag up "Hey guys, we're not really being effective in mission". In a small church, if the leadership team do not organise themselves to ask how mission is going on a regular basis, nothing happens!

It is helpful for churches of any size to have a framework for mission activities and to communicate the purpose of each activity to everyone within the church. A good framework is explained in the book *Sowing, Reaping, Keeping* which suggests that any evangelistic activity can be measured on a scale of 0–10 (the Engle Scale): 0 being where a person knows nothing about God and 10 is a person deciding to follow Jesus.

From 1–3 on the scale, there are Sowing 1 activities which show visitors that God is good and Christians are OK. From 4–6 Sowing 2 activities contain a gospel presentation which may be completely new to many. From 7–8 (Reaping 1) the conversation will introduce the implications of following Jesus and the cost of the gospel. From 9–10 (Reaping 2) there will be an opportunity to make a decision to become a Christian. As we move people up the scale from 0 towards 10, the number of people usually gets fewer. 'Keeping' includes ways of keeping and encouraging new Christians.

This framework should give encouragement to many churches who have engaged in mission but have not seen people converted. Moving people up the scale of awareness of who God is, is essential work. By using this scale and framework, it enables the expectation of any activity to be on target. A sowing activity should not be expected to have the same result as a reaping activity. Laurence Singlehurst writes:

> I was involved in a church that at great expense had rented the largest theatre in town and put on an ambitious Christmas pantomime. The theatre was full to capacity and every night over sixty percent of the audiences were non-Christians. Yet at the end of their run the church was devastated because no one in the audience had actually been converted. Once again we can see that this was a great sowing strategy, but they had expected the results of a reaping one. No wonder they were disappointed.[1]

In the Tools section of this chapter, there are examples of mission activity in each of *Sowing, Reaping, Keeping's* categories.

The Missional Nature of a Smaller Church – by Dan Yarnell, Baptist Union Specialist Mission Networker for Smaller Churches

> "The greatest hermeneutic[2] of the gospel is the local church". Bishop Lesslie Newbigin

Small churches are most often found on the frontline of mission today. This may sound like a bold statement, but you will find

---

[1] Laurence Singlehurst, *Sowing, Reaping, Keeping* – used with permission.

[2] Hermeneutics is the art or science of interpretation, especially of Scripture.

them as new church plants, fresh expressions of being church, or for most, enduring communities of faithful worshippers in city centres, suburbs, villages and among various people groups all over this country and the world. The commitment to faithfully express the good news with seemingly little resource (especially the lack of people) is remarkable.

One of the key terms that is being bantered about today is the word missional. It is primarily a reminder to us that God is first and foremost a missionary (after all, he loved the world and sent his only Son, who came under the power of the Spirit). This however is not just some new term we add to the church, like a new piece of wallpaper adhered to a cracked and peeling surface. Nor is it a term for new expressions of church or even key events that relate to the missionary nature of the church. These are already happening and often seeing some fruit.

Missional is more about the recognition that the world we live in has and is changing at a rapid rate. Unlike Dorothy in the Wizard of Oz who only wanted to go home to Kansas, there is for us no going home, no going back to the world that was. This stark reality means that to be effective and faithful requires a new way of imagining what church could mean to a changed world.

Alan Roxbrough, an Englishman who lives and works in Canada, is one of the voices who is assisting churches to focus on a few of the key issues that are involved in considering being missional. In his freely downloadable booklet *What is Missional Church?* (www.allelon.org) he highlights the following as key issues in the understanding of what it means to be missional:

1. Western Society as a mission field. We are no longer primarily the sender of missionaries to the developing world, but rather the recipient of missionaries to assist us in engaging the culture of the West, which has either forgotten or is uninterested in our Christian past. We are all called to be missionaries to our world, often our work colleagues, our neighbours, our friends.

2. Mission is about the *Missio Dei*. God is a missionary, the Bible is a missionary document, and the church must express this aspect of the nature of God to be fully authentic as a faith community. This means the focus is mostly outward (go into the world) rather than inward (come to us). Allowing God to take us on a journey with Him.

3. A different society. Peter in his first epistle reminds the small, scattered Christian communities he writes to that they are a peculiar people. This does not mean they are odd (although some are), but rather they live by a different set of values which will often lead to conflict with the world (and its competing values). Becoming a church community that authentically lives by the values of the Kingdom of God demonstrates a new way of living life to a watching world.

The reality for many smaller churches is primarily one of survival. Can we yet live? Sometimes this is stated as: "we need to keep the door open". By this it usually means we need more people like us to keep this ship afloat. However, survival cannot be the main reason for its existence. The core question must become "can this small church become missional?" For without engaging in this process, the small church will surrender its engagement with God in his mission and eventually become focused primarily on maintenance as its primary reason to exist.

There are ways that smaller churches are often already missional. These include:

- New church plants
- Fresh expressions of being church
- First generation churches to various ethnic and people groups
- Persecuted churches

In all these expressions of church, mission is at the heart or the church would cease to exist. In all of these experiences, these churches have faced up to the considerable challenges and obstacles that hinder them in their missional journey.

I honestly believe that small churches can become missional communities. There are, however, serious obstacles that can and do prevent this. These include:

1. Fear

It is quite a common occurrence that God's people often express fear in their encounter with him. However, that type of fear does not paralyze them in moving towards obedience. The fear I am speaking about overwhelms so that it becomes intimidating to faith and action. It may take many forms but underneath it all is the need to change and the inability to do so. If fear can be overcome, then faith can arise and something new can come forth. This usually involves trust.

2. Tradition

A lot of tradition is very good. It expresses the framework of how God has been at work among this group of people. We usually do things because someone somewhere considered this a good way of expressing our belief and behaviour. Tradition can however become debilitating and its own task master. It can sap energy as another form of maintenance. Many new forms of church have found re-examining earlier expressions of tradition as an aid in their spiritual journey. By discovering the original intent of these expressions, tradition can become an empowering tool in rediscovering a freshness in worship and mission.

3. Security

There is a fact of life that the older we get, the more we like things to be comfortable. While our security needs to be in God, often it is in our current understanding or the limits of involvement with Him that provide security. Security is good, safety, however, is questionable. Healthy churches should be safe places where people can be themselves and explore together their faith. But safety can prevent us from taking the risks that faith demand. The few who wish to engage missionally will find security not in safety, but rather in the God who journeys with them to all the hard places where the love of God needs to be demonstrated and experienced.

4. Experiences

The Bible is full of stories of people encountering God. Often these experiences have totally transformed their lives. So experience can be a good teacher. But many in smaller churches have had difficult and traumatic experiences, often by good intentioned people or ides, which have left them uncertain and untrusting of the stories of others. Often by retelling both the Biblical stories and the original faith stories of the founders of the church, along with current faith building stories, the previous memories can be erased or at least limited to allow a new openness to try something new.

5. Theology

What we believe does affect what we do and how we live. Honest exploration in study can be liberating and empowering. Rediscovering who God is, what he is about and how he is at work is always worth exploring. In the same way, bad theology will hamper and ultimately destroy the very thing that was intended in the first place. We still need the teachers and educators who will assist us in thinking and exploring how our faith is made real.

6. People

This is the reality of church, the very people who make up the body. Helpful people will aid us in our mission like nothing else, unhelpful ones will hinder us. We are all sinners who are under the grace of God, so none of us has got it all sorted out. However, we do need to discover how to work together to express being the church today in our new context. We also need those outside of our immediate context that will aid us on the journey. Learning to be the body of Christ is one of the most missional endeavours we can provide to a watching world. Expressing the character of God, the reality of Jesus, the power of the Spirit provides a reality like no other.

All of these can and will stop the church from fully engaging in its mission. However, I also believe that with the right help, all of these can be turned into assets that will foster the process of re-imagining a new way to be the church.

Revelation chapters 2 and 3 reminds us that each of the seven churches mentioned had good and bad, helpful and unhelpful elements to its life. The prophetic voice of Jesus was given to enable the church to once again see its potential, to once again join him in the missional journey. But they needed to repent; to change directions; to go again with him in trust and obedience, or they would fail and cease to exist.

This is our challenge: to follow God where He leads us, to the people and opportunities that a changing world presents us. We cannot go back to a previous generation or time, we must learn from them and move forward. We need the help of others to take the first steps. We need to surrender the church back to Him, and let Him speak His word of truth to us. And if we listen and follow, then we can join Him again in the journey of mission that He is taking in our world today.

Mission in the Community

Mission can be done by one church or, more powerfully, by a group of churches working together to reach a locality, town or village. Mission has a broad spectrum and includes major projects such as Soul in the City, Festival Manchester or "On The Move" Missions. There is a place for proclamation evangelism but when surveys have been done, more people come to Christ through friendship evangelism, as people bring their friends, neighbours and workmates along. Mission also includes befriending the marginalised and loving the unloved, offering the gospel alongside a bowl of soup or a blanket.

> Canonbury Community Baptist Church in London with 12 members meet in and run a Community Centre, manage a befriending project, provide lunches for 25 older people every day and co-ordinate other groups which use the building. Once a month they invite people to a Sunday lunch which is followed by a church service at 2pm. During the average week they have quality contact with over 50 local people.

It can be hard work, showing Jesus' love to those who have learnt not to trust anyone. It can personally cost to reach out, but to see Jesus transform lives through the power of the Spirit and rescue people from an eternity in hell makes it all worthwhile.

Mission Overseas

The recognition of overseas mission is important for any church not just so a global perspective can be maintained, but because many of the exciting advances of the Christian faith are taking place overseas. Interest and response from church members is always higher if there is a personal connection. Sponsoring the education of the children in a village is a good way for individuals, groups or small churches to be involved. People are called from churches of all sizes to serve overseas in mission or relief work and their regular news updates and photographs can be an inspiration and encouragement to those serving at home. Twinning with churches overseas is referred to in Chapter 7. Because of the value difference in exchange rates, a small church raising a small amount of money can finance a major outreach programme in some parts of the world.

Mission Budget

It is good practice for a church to have a budget for mission, perhaps separated between home and overseas work. This keeps the work of mission as a priority and avoids the situation where any-thing left when all the other bills are paid is spent on mission! Investing in resources to make Jesus known is always good value.

> Zion Chapel run a ladies social evening (friendship evangel-ism/sowing). On one occasion 32 ladies came to learn how to make Christmas decorations. Of these, 10 had no chapel links. As the cash flow is a bit tight at the chapel, the social evenings are funded by a 50p a week donation from each member. All 16 members are pensioners but they will not let money get in the way of mission.

Who do we reach, Where and How?

The who, where, and how to reach with the gospel will probably change over time as God leads the church into new areas of experience. The church needs to have a heart for the community, which flows more naturally if they live there rather than commute. Because the people, energy and resources are limited in a small church, asking God what the specific area of mission is to be is essential. Prayer meetings just for this purpose can be inspiring. An idea is to pray over a map asking God where to start – a geographical area, a collection of streets, an estate or a postal code area. It is always helpful to research the area using the latest census information or better still, meet people with a door to door survey.

People Group – God may point out a people group or need to reach rather than an area, such as 0–5 year olds, single parents, young, old, people struggling with addictions, unemployed etc.

God's heart is for the widows and orphans . . . "Religion that God our Father accepts as pure and faultless is this: to look after orphans and widows in their distress and to keep oneself from being polluted by the world" (James 1v27 NIV). . . . the poor and the lonely . . . "A father to the fatherless, a defender of widows, is God

101

in his holy dwelling. God sets the lonely in families, he leads forth the prisoners with singing" (Psalms 68v5–6 NIV). . . . and the marginalised, such as immigrants, homeless, asylum seekers, mentally handicapped and vagrants.

He calls us to bring Kingdom values like trust, truth, moral standards, forgiveness and reconciliation back to our world that have been tossed aside. Our major task though, is to get the message known that people can be rescued from an eternity in hell.

Don't Despair!

The purpose of bridge building or mission is to bring people within earshot of the call of Christ. We may do the planting and watering but it is Christ through his Holy Spirit who converts, if we do our work, the Spirit can do His. Much of our work is sowing, but often others do the reaping at a later date. We are called to go out, not to be "successful".

Small Church + Big Vision = Impact in the Community
by Rev. Frank Brookes, Rayleigh Park Baptist Church

My personal theme verse is: "But God chose the foolish things of the world to shame the wise; God chose the weak things of the world to shame the strong" (1 Corinthians 1v27 NIV).

I was brought up in a coal mining community near Rotherham and followed my Father and Grandfather into the job. I got into a bad lifestyle in my early 20s which finished up with me being sent to prison for drug pushing. When I was about 23, Arthur Blessit came to Birmingham to hold evangelistic meetings and there I committed my life to Christ. I moved to Cornwall, working as a plumbing and heating engineer and attended Redruth Baptist Church. At 29 or 30, I joined an organisation called Operation Mobilisation which has two missionary ships, The Logos and The Doulos. I worked with them for 23 years as a missionary, conference speaker and prison visitor in South America and Asia. I met up with Arthur Blessit again in India and was able to spend a month with him.

In 1997 I studied at Spurgeon's College to train for church ministry and came to Rayleigh Park Baptist Church, as a part-time student in 2000 (I am still part-time now). I found that a small church was hard work in areas such as worship, Sunday School and church meetings.

The rebirth and vision of Rayleigh Park came primarily through prayer meetings held on Monday nights for 5 years by the church leadership. However, it was on one Saturday afternoon, God clearly directed us to five needs in our community:

1. Drugs
2. Abortion
3. Prison
4. Prostitutes
5. Arabic Muslims

How are we seeking to meet these community needs?

1. Drugs – There used to be much freedom in Brixton to use drugs. I discovered in 2004 that the police were turning a blind eye to soft drug users to look at the short-term effect on our local estate. The church approached the Christian Lawyers Fellowship and together took the local Chief of Police to court. It soon became national news and there was much media coverage. There is now a new Chief of Police and a No Tolerance to Drugs policy adopted. We are now building good relationships with our local police. The lesson learnt is to be prepared to challenge those in authority if it is felt that what they are doing is wrong. Having said that we should always remember to pray for them and support them in the good work that they do. The church has started a ministry called TRANSFORM to reach out to ex-addicts and pushers.

2. Abortion – There is an Abortion clinic building next to the church, which has carried out over 50,000 abortions since 1970.

I was wondering about this issue when I was challenged by two Catholic ladies asking what a church was doing next door to an abortion clinic! I was convicted of our inaction and with the church, watched the harrowing video called *The Silent Scream*. A lot of us cried. The church wanted to reach out to the women next door but how? We didn't want to be aggressive or fanatical about it, so we plan to start a pregnancy crisis centre opening two or three times a week. In 2007, we are extending this service to include a Pro-Life course called IMAGE and run by Pro-Life professionals. We again enlisted the help of the Christian Lawyers Fellowship when an extension to the Clinic was proposed, and together we led an active and successful community campaign against it.

3. Prison – The church lies in the shadow of Brixton prison, which holds nearly 1000 prisoners. I regularly visit prisons to share the gospel with the inmates. Four years ago, I visited Swaleside Prison and shared my testimony with about 70 men. When I asked my usual question "Does anyone come from Brixton?" some hands went up. Afterwards, a prisoner named Steve talked to me and asked if I would could contact a member of his family. I discovered that he had become a Christian while in prison and I agreed with the proviso that he came to visit my church on his release. Amazingly, Steve who had been inside for 13 years for pushing crack arrived at the church one Sunday morning. We helped him to get a job in Peckham with a government funded local church's initiative to find jobs for the locally unemployed. Steve now helps ex-offenders to find work and accommodation. We started a meeting once a month for ex-offenders run by ex-offenders at our church, and is also attended by the Chaplain of Brixton Prison and the leader of the Prison Christian Fellowships. Some attendees, like Steve, are strong Christians and are asked to speak at national events. Rayleigh Park takes teams of ex-offenders to other churches to speak and have had airtime on Premier Radio and the God Channel.

4. Prostitution – In the summer of 2005, we invited an ex-prostitute to come and work among the local girls in Brixton. We really need a team to work in the local red light district (about 70 girls in Brixton Hill). Behind prostitution are the crack dealers and there is a crack house nearby. We admit we are weak in this area of specialised ministry and are seeking ways to build the work.

5. Arabic Muslim Community – There is a rising number of people from Iran, Iraq, Morocco, Tunisia and Egypt living in Brixton. We have set up a coffee bar in the afternoons on Monday to Friday, where people from all nations relax and chat to half a dozen church volunteers about life issues. In 2003 we invited the local lively and growing English/Arabic speaking church to meet on our premises and approximately 30 people come to the service each Sunday at 4pm.

Our small church of just 21 members, working together as a team has baptised ex-prostitutes and ex-heroine addicts and we have seen many freed from their addictions to drugs and alcohol. We are still struggling with issues such as finance, reliable volunteers, administration and lack of counsellors. BUT God is slowly fulfilling this BIG vision and choosing to use us! Praise His name!

Using the *Jesus* Video Project by Rev. David Priddy, Ashford Common Baptist Church (formerly Napier Road Christian Fellowship)

At Napier Road Christian Fellowship we saw an opportunity to take the good news of Jesus beyond the walls of our community hall by distributing the *Jesus* video. The video was available at just £1 per copy and was fully supported by leaflets, ideas and other resources. (The film is still available in both VHS and DVD formats from Agape on 0121 765 4404.)

After prayer and a little planning, a few of our members went to the roads immediately around our meeting place to offer free copies of the video to those who were interested. An integral part of the project is that each house taking a video is revisited and the householder asked a series of questions on their opinion of the video itself. These questions lead towards an opportunity to ask if the viewer prayed the prayer of commitment at the end of the video.

We found a mixed response. Some roads had a high take up rate, but elsewhere the response was disappointing. No one joined our church as a result of the project, but we did not see it as a failure – we sow the seeds and God produces the harvest.

The seeds were not simply sown in the houses we visited. We talked about the project in the Thames Valley District of the London Baptist Association and with other Baptist Churches. The result was that several other churches took up the project. We designed and delivered two training courses for them: one as a motivational course focusing on the need to share the good news with our neighbours and the other as a how to do it event. Our small church has a ministry beyond ourselves.

The church has always been actively involved in the local Churches Together group. As we talked with our colleagues about the project and its potential, it was felt that God was leading the six churches to conduct a project over a somewhat larger area. Plans were made for the distribution to be targeted at the TW16 postcode area and phased over a couple of years. It was agreed that we would only start the project if all the churches joined in and a sign of God's anointing was seen as all six signed-up. Some churches committed to pray for the project, others committed to offer the videos to householders.

Training events were held for each church co-ordinator and participant, then the project was launched with a joint commissioning service involving all 6 churches. We were taking the good news into our surrounding area. The project continued for 2 years, with all churches continuing to be committed to it (albeit to varying degrees) with 3,881 homes visited and 483 videos distributed.

So what did the project achieve?

Firstly, the planning and the execution of the project was a major catalyst in bringing the 6 churches closer together. Despite changes of leadership in 4 of the churches, the spirit of co-operation and fellowship has continued to this day. Secondly, it has raised the profile of the Church in the area. One significant feature was that each householder received a letter about the video before being offered one. The letter was signed by the Leaders of each church: two Anglican Churches, a Roman Catholic Church, a Methodist church, a Newfrontiers Church and a Baptist Church. Several members of the public commented on this visible sign of churches working together. Thirdly, and most importantly, several people made first time commitments to Christ and have joined local churches.

MISSION TOOLS

Sowing, Reaping, Keeping **Framework**

Examples of a balanced mission strategy – reproduced by permission.

Sowing 1	Sowing 2	Reaping	Keeping
Lunch Club for Elderly	Afternoon tea & talk	Faith Rediscovered Course	Discussion/ Bible group Sunday Service
Parent & Toddlers Group	Parenting Class based on Christian principles	Parent & Children Service	Kidz Club & Parents' Discussion Group Sunday Service
Quiz Night	Meal with a Gospel message	Just Looking course	Home Groups Sunday Service

Sowing 1 Activity

To meet people in a social context and through conversation get over that Christians are OK and God is good.

Sowing 2 Activity

Present the gospel in a relevant way.

Reaping Activity

Discussion around the Christian faith with a decision opportunity.

Keeping Activity

A suitable group to enhance belonging and get to know other church members.

Ideas for Mission in the Community

Sowing 1

- Barbecues in local park – free food and entertainment for locals.
- Big screen live showings of sports events such as The World Cup, Wimbledon, Olympics.
- Day trips such as seaside, park, country rambles.
- Gardening demonstration.
- Welcome packs to new neighbours.
- Quiz night.
- Meet a community need in your building – washing facilities/ Parent and Toddlers/coffee shop/toy library/lunches etc.
- Coffee morning.
- English language classes – one church became a UK Online Centre, taught English as a second language and soon became a centre for asylum seekers and other foreign people to meet socially.

Sowing 2

- Give away free gospels.
- Free Christian newspapers such as *Challenge* or London City Mission's *Good News Paper*.
- Meals with a meaning – good food at a local restaurant and Christian speaker/entertainer; each Christian brings a non-Christian friend; a good book to give out is *Dinner with a Perfect Stranger* by David Gregory (published by Hodder & Stoughton 2005).
- Parenting classes.
- *Jesus* video project.
- Afternoon tea and talk.

Reaping

- Just Looking groups.

109

- Alpha/Christianity Explored/Emmaus courses.[1]
- Seeker services.
- Faith Rediscovered course.[1]
- Lunch and gospel presentation.
- Y Course.[1]

Keeping

- Discussion/ Bible group.
- Sunday service.
- Basic Christianity course.
- Link with prayer partner or "buddy".

Small Group Activity – Mission Challenge

(A) You have £50 to spend. You have 2 able-bodied workers besides yourself, and another 4 members who are elderly, two of whom have limited mobility.

Plan an outreach activity, either as a one-off event or a weekly meeting, to reach:

1. over 65s.
2. children under 12.
3. working couples.

(B) You have £150 to spend. You have 4 able-bodied workers besides yourself and another 10 members who are either elderly and disabled or not very willing to be involved.

Plan an outreach activity, either as a one-off event or a weekly meeting to reach:

1. teenagers.
2. young families.
3. people with learning difficulties.

---

[1] Small churches often work together with other local churches to run courses.

(C) You have £500 to spend. You have 1 able-bodied worker besides yourself and 2 reasonably mobile and active elderly ladies.

Plan an event or activity which will reach out to the community immediately surrounding the church.

How to tell others your story – Personal Testimony

Telling others our testimony (not just the story of how we became a Christian but the activity of God in our lives in both large and small ways) may be something that we are not used to doing. The best way to overcome nerves or being tongue-tied, is to practice with other Christians. People enjoy listening to personal, real life stories, the weekly magazines are living proof! Practice telling your story in 4 easy sections:

- What was my attitude before I took Jesus Christ seriously?
- Why I said Yes to Jesus?
- How did I say Yes to Jesus?
- What difference does knowing Jesus make to my everyday life?

If coming to Christ was not at a specific time or place but more of a gradual process, these questions may be more appropriate for you to use:

- What were 1 or 2 things that use to characterise my view of life?
- Why do I still want to put Jesus first in my life?
- Were there any particular points in my life when I reinforced my earlier decision to say Yes to Jesus?
- What difference does Jesus make in my everyday life?

Some useful hints about telling your story:

- Use familiar words and ideas that people can understand. Avoid jargon or Christian-sounding words or phrases e.g. use forgiver instead of saviour, leader instead of Lord.

111

- Be specific. Mention a real detail, incident, place, thought, feeling or statement. Avoid being vague.
- Be honest. Don't exaggerate, or cover up weaknesses or tough situations – they help people identify with you and add credibility.
- Don't mention church denominations, especially in a negative way and be cautious of talking about church. Point people to Christ, not institutional Christianity.
- Make each section short and to the point.

When practised, you can adapt the testimony to emphasise points that each individual listener can identify with. Also practise having everyday conversations and find a way to introduce your testimony. This means that when a situation arises, you will be relaxed, confident and not phased by a question from a friend or acquaintance.

Questions about Mission

This is a list of questions to be discussed by the Leadership and/or in small groups

- Is mission a priority? Is growth a priority?
- Jesus said "Go". Look at mission in your church; are you going or are you saying "come", or a mixture of both?
- What sowing, reaping, and keeping activities are your church involved in?
- How many people have committed their lives to Christ in the last 5 years as a result of mission activity?
- Are people happy to tell others about their faith, or would practice help?
- Have you engaged in area-wide mission with other local churches? Would you like to?
- Is there a specific group of people your church has been asked to reach? Do you need outside help or more information to reach them better? Do you produce leaflets in a variety of languages?

- Is there a budget for mission? Have you thought of applying for funding? There is help available from a variety of sources depending on the project (see Chapter 9).
- Are you involved in mission or supporting mission overseas?

Can the Small Reach Out to All?

"We seemed like grasshoppers in our own eyes, and we looked the same to them" (Numbers 13v33). The reaction of 10 spies Moses sent into Canaan sums up how a small church often feels when faced with the task of reaching a large local community. We can easily get discouraged, feel we are outnumbered and also get the impression that no one is interested in Christianity any more. 1 Peter 2v11–12 and Ephesians 2v12 paint a dark picture of those who don't yet know Jesus, but we should not assume this means those outside the church have no faith or belief.

Faith in the Community
Almost 70% of people in opinion polls still say they believe in God and many claim to belong to a church. What is missing is the connection between those outside the church and those inside the church.

What Sort of Faith?
Aside from those who have a knowledgeable belief in a particular religion, there are sizeable groups of those who have:

Residual Faith – a deposit of belief left from childhood involvement in Sunday School or Bible clubs. Often vague, it may emerge after many years when there is a crisis, or in conversation with church-goers.

Insurance Faith – almost a superstition rather than a real belief. It makes people want babies christened, church weddings and religious funerals, for their own reassurance.

113

Pick and Mix Faith – bits of doctrine, ideas, fantasy and spirituality all mixed together. No clear belief system, people are seeking meaning in their lives but are unable to sort out the wide variety of religions on offer.

How do we re-connect with people living around our church?
1. Meeting their needs by providing services. We can set up groups/ clubs/meetings which meet a need in the community – Mums and Toddlers, Children's Club, Youth Club, Over 60s etc. These reach out and encourage people to come to the church building, and we pray that they will not only enjoy the activity but start asking questions and finding answers.

The problems with this method is that the responsibility for crossing the bridge between community and church lies with the people outside the church. No church can build enough bridges to reach every age group and lifestyle. A small church may only have the resources for 1 or 2 bridges. Is this the best way to invest limited manpower and money?

2. Becoming Bridges
Step 1 – All members learn to see themselves as a bridge into the community, recognising family, friends, colleagues, neighbours as people who are likely to have some form of faith but have not connected yet with the church and Jesus.

Step 2 – As a deliberate outreach strategy, leaders and members each get involved in one or two community activities such as adult education, hobbies, clubs, sport, dance classes, coffee mornings, bingo, pub quiz teams. Whatever they will really enjoy and will put them where they can build friendships with non-churchgoers. The members and leaders become bridges and cross the gap into the church alongside the seeker, instead of standing at the church end of the bridge and shouting to people to come across.

Challenges we may face

Shyness and lack of confidence – this places a lot of responsibility on individual members. Doing it in pairs (New Testament style) may be best.

Need for Prayer – members will need focused prayer for those they meet and befriend – this could be done during Sunday worship.

Discouragement – This kind of "presence evangelism" can take months or years before friendships are really established and people can be invited to outreach events or courses. Discouragement may set in as it is harder to see the results of this method than the church-run groups and clubs method and hence it is important to set expectations that this is firstly a Sowing activity (see the *Sowing, Reaping, Keeping* framework).

Useful Bible references

God cares about and reaches out to people outside the church: Psalm 145v9–12; Romans 1v18–20; Acts 17v26–28.

Jesus' ministry was church and community based, motivated by compassion: Matthew 9v1, 9–10, 35–38.

Questions for Discussion and Reflection

- What signs of faith or searching for God have you seen in family/friends/colleagues who don't attend church? How could you make use of these signs of faith to draw people towards Jesus?
- How much of your spare time (members) or ministry (leaders) is spent with Christians and how much with non-Christians? Do you need to change your priorities?
- Could the Becoming Bridges outreach strategy be used in your church? What would have to change to make this happen?

GROWTH AND CHANGE IN A SMALL CHURCH

> But the LORD says, "Do not cling to events of the past or dwell on what happened long ago. Watch for the new thing I am going to do. It is happening already – you can see it now! I will make a road through the wilderness and give you streams of water there. (Isaiah 43v18–19 TEV)

Being engaged in mission usually brings an exciting opportunity called **change!** People cope with change differently; some embrace it, some resist it and some endure it. Before embarking on a mission activity, the possible change it may bring must be understood by all. Growth to the Kingdom is always a cause for celebration, but growth in a small church could mean that things will never be the same again. Understanding will hopefully open hearts to welcome new people. Some changes that happen may be:

- The "culture" will change.
- The small family feel goes.
- Relationships will not be as close with everyone as they used to be.
- Maybe resistance to give old jobs to new people.
- "Invasion" of people group i.e. children, older people, ethnic group, which change the church dynamics.
- Less easy to be flexible and making decisions quickly.
- Can take a long time for new people to settle in.
- Steep learning curve with new people with new problems not previously encountered by the church.
- Leadership has less time for the regulars while helping the new people through basic courses/pastoral time.

Forewarned is forearmed but keep in view that there is a celebration in heaven every time a sinner repents, so join the party!

Change also takes place when the way things are done just don't make sense any more, or when a minister leaves or significant people leave or die, so a continuation of the ministry looks impossible. This calls for new ways of doing things or new people to do them.

> If you want something you've never had before, you'll have to do something you've never done before.

Change happens as a result of desperation and the results are often surprising and pleasing and the question "why didn't we do this before?" is asked. It is said that small churches have a choice . . . evolution or revolution!

> There was a small church with a generally older congregation and a few children who didn't attend every Sunday due to parental visiting rights. They had to think their way around what they did in a Sunday service. Half an hour sermons caused some of the older folks to sleep, or to sigh and grunt as sitting in one position became painful. Children's Sunday School materials were designed for larger groups and followed on consecutively. They were spending a fortune on teacher's notes and children's magazines with loads going to waste. Something had to change! After praying about the problem, they had a radical re-structuring of the Sunday service to include all ages in interactive worship.

Sunday Services

Sunday services have to be relevant to each congregation and be led sensitively. In society, life has changed so that the occasions where people sit and listen to a person speaking to them for half an hour or more, are very few and far between. Lessons in schools are interactive and meetings in the workplace contain discussion and presentations. TV has pictures to illustrate even the heaviest of documentaries. People come into church and we expect them to feel at ease in a very alien environment. It is important to know if people in the church have difficulties of any sort and be sensitive to their needs during the service.

> One small church said "We don't have a sermon as such any more but the teaching is broken into 3 or 4 smaller sections. We use lots of OHP graphics, large pictures, artefacts, taped music and discussion. (It would be useful to have PowerPoint and also use video clips but it is expensive and we can't justify that money)." The congregation have said that they now enjoy the services much more and because they are doing and seeing, remember much more too. For our church this model works very well and is much more relevant than the traditional "hymn, prayer, sermon sandwich".

From 9 Members to 93 in Four Years! How? by Tade Agbesanwa, Custom House Baptist Church, London

Custom House Baptist Church in the East End of London was started in 1906 and as is witnessed by the old minute books, has had its ups and downs over the years, but its real problems started about 12 years ago when its congregation was weakened by the departure of the Ascension Church (Church of England) back to its own renovated building. Custom House had relied heavily on them to lead the worship and they also made a significant contribution in helping with the preaching and teaching.

When they left, a couple of active young members also left, perhaps because of the links developed with the Ascension leadership and the attraction of a new building. Other families were also leaving the church; especially the African and Caribbean families who went on to join the many new Pentecostal churches springing up in the area.

The problems were further exacerbated by persistent vandalism and a major arson attack on the church building. As can be imagined, this drained the finances of an already struggling church, and sadly under these pressures, church meetings were very contentious and draining and leadership became stressful. During this period the church had two pastors, but eventually one and then the other had to leave as the church could not afford to pay them and a Home Mission grant was not forthcoming.

Things got worse when both the Financial Secretary and Treasurer left. The Fabric Secretary (an informal church leader) also resigned and nominated me to become Church Leader but later changed his mind. I however remained church leader.

Eventually, a lot of resentment broke out about the direction in which the church life was moving. Several of the older members thought the character of the church had changed both in terms of ethnicity, how worship was led and how leadership was carried out. There were walkouts during church services, refusals to take part in communion or join in prayer, openly reading newspapers during the sermon etc. It was a big mess for a small church with only about 15 in attendance on an average Sunday. Soon after, six members including a prominent family of four adults also left the church. This was a severe blow as this family had worked extremely hard to make sure the church kept its doors open and the fellowship were heavily dependent on them. The church was now down to nine members and Sunday mornings were hard and discouraging with rows and rows of empty seats.

Eventually 4 of the remaining church members decided to join together in prayer for the church. It was during this time of prayer and brainstorming that one of us mentioned *The Purpose Driven Church* by Rick Warren of Saddleback Church, California. We studied the book extensively and held weekly meetings to discuss how the book might be relevant to our church. This led to defining a vision for the church and spelling out our 5 purposes: Worship, Fellowship, Discipleship, Ministry and Mission. Through God's help, the church's life was reordered using these purposes.

Worship

- Worship is far more than music but one of the things we did was to buy a new, versatile keyboard that could be programmed to play many instruments as we were a very small church and had only a small pool of musical talent to draw from.
- We changed our PA system as the one we had gave out very poor quality sound. We were able to purchase these because we had another church using our premises and they paid us a rent. We also had a day-care centre that paid rent to us.
- The worship area was repainted in a lighter colour, and the old choir stall removed to give the feel of a more open church. We replaced a lot of the old fluorescent lighting to give a brighter feel to the church.
- Generous flower arrangements were placed in the worship area (unfortunately we've now stepped down to artificial flowers!)
- We bought a video projector to take advantage of the many films now available to enhance worship and to use for sermon illustration.
- The old grey carpet was replaced with a red one to match the chairs.
- Upbeat music was played in the background or a praise and worship DVD projected on screen about 15 minutes before the service started. We did this to put visitors in a celebratory mood.
- We try to make our communion service (once a month) special. We usually have Taizé music playing in the background while video clips relevant to the service play on the big screen.
- We have introduced sermon notes which make the sermons easier to follow, especially for those who are not regular church attendees. It is also something to study later at home.

Fellowship

Hospitality – We set out to make our visitors welcome so that they would come back again, but often found they didn't return for several reasons.

One of the things we had to invest heavily in was our toilets. They were cold and waterlogged most of the time. There was no toilet paper or air freshener, the air extractor didn't work and lighting was poor. Some of the doors didn't shut properly. We also upgraded the heating system as it constantly broke down in winter.

In order to encourage people to stay after the service we introduced a good selection of snacks after the church service. This gave the leaders a chance to meet visitors and have a conversation. This has now grown into what we call Café 3:16. Hopefully this will grow into a fresh expression of church.

Visibility – One of the questions we asked ourselves was "How would an outsider passing by see our church?" the answer was "They don't even see us!" We were simply zoned out of people's minds. Indeed the taxi driver from the cab office next to our church who had been there for 3 years didn't know our church!

- We painted the outside of the church white. This was to show the community the church was very much alive and well. We removed the graffiti and replaced the wall behind the church with more open fencing.
- We changed name to "The House" and have a red plaque on the door that shows this new name. Officially of course we're still Custom House Baptist Church.
- We put a huge poster outside the church with an "I believe" theme, which has been very effective.
- Last Christmas we had the nativity scene in lights outside of the church. It was a very lovely sight at night and again had passers by pausing.
- At the time of writing, we have erected a huge, un-missable cross in the front yard of the church to mark the Lenten period. We just might leave it out there for a while yet.
- I sometimes sweep the yard in front of the church and take opportunities to talk to passers by and invite them in.

- We have flowerpots in front of the church to make it more appealing to casual observers and usually have the topic of the sermon on our notice board most times.
- Outings – Custom House Baptist Church has frequent outings to theme parks, concerts, drama productions etc. We also hold annual Women and Men's breakfasts. This has been a good way of inviting friends and family into the life of the church which has worked very well.

The result has been that many people have come in and become part of the life of the church.

Discipleship

One of the key elements that God used to grow our church was the "40 days of Purpose" discipleship programme, again by Rick Warren. Apart from the content of the course, the process of putting it together galvanised the church. A lot of people, who were uncommitted to the church, committed themselves. People volunteered to serve in various ministries, giving went up, friends were invited to church etc.

The church no longer runs the "40 days of Purpose" as a church wide campaign but it continues in its small group version.

Ministry

One of the key ministries that we believe has been instrumental to our growth has been the children's ministry. So many parents have said they've stayed because their children enjoyed Sunday school so much (and I thought it was my sermons!).

The children are not present during the sermon and response part of the service as adults find this distracting but they are present at the praise and worship segment.

Mission (Evangelism)

The emphasis on mission in our church has been to friends and family. We have tried community outreach but the results are uncertain. Uncertain because we don't ask if people have come to church because they got our invitation card through our door-to-door campaigns or simply walked in.

One of the tools we have used for our friends and family outreach efforts has been the "Becoming a Contagious Christian" course from Willow Creek Community Church in the USA. This has worked very well.

We have also recently introduced the "Marriage Preparation" and "Marriage" courses to the church and already have six non-church couples waiting to do either course.

What has been the result of all this?

In terms of numbers, the church has grown from 9 members to 93 in about 4 years. We have also had 10 baptisms in the same period with about 9 more due after Easter 2007. Again, the majority of those baptised have been friends and family.

Average attendance on a Sunday has settled to just over 100 but a majority of our members come only twice a month because they have to work Sundays on a rotation basis. This is a blessing of sorts as we have a small building and would not be able to fit everyone in.

The church continues to grow spiritually as well as numerically and the atmosphere is one of joy and peace, a far cry from what it was a few years ago. We give thanks and praise to God alone!

"It's About Following Jesus Together" by Rev. Sandra Thwaites, North Hanwell Baptist Church, London

If we must speak of numbers then four-and-a-half years ago if there were 18 in the congregation on a Sunday morning, that would have been deemed "a really good week". Now? We average 60–65. People of all ages, married, single, co-habiting, divorced, babies, children, young people, young, middle-aged, old, black, white and Asian. Folk of all backgrounds. Some have known Jesus as Lord for longer than I've been alive, some have just encountered

Him and others are curious. But each one of us is on a journey – together. About eight years ago, as I was reading Isaiah, and God seemed to highlight 41v18–20!

> ". . . I will turn the desert into pools of water, and the parched ground into springs. I will put in the desert the cedar and the acacia, the myrtle and the olive. I will set pines in the wasteland, the fir and cypress together, so that people may see and know, may consider and understand, that the hand of The Lord has done this, that The Holy One of Israel has created it."

You know, it's impossible for those plants and trees to grow together. They each need different soils, temperatures, irrigation etc. But that's God's Church! People who shouldn't or wouldn't be together – are!

It also underlines the difficulty I have in saying how we have built-up the church community at North Hanwell, because it really is God at work! It's as though He's rolling out a red carpet (because we're royalty) in front of us. Just a little at a time, and we walk on the carpet step by step. We have no plans for the next year, let alone the next two or five. We're just trusting our Lord to take us, and use us as His Kingdom comes to The Cuckoo Estate.

That said, there are, I think, some general principals and golden rules to "growing". It's nothing new, it's stuff we all know, but we can so easily lose sight of. In our wanting to get bigger, see folk brought into the Kingdom, lives changed etc. we become impatient. When Jesus said "I will build My Church" He meant it! It's His, not ours. And He always keeps His Word, so He will build it! We're called to follow. It's not a programme, it's not the latest fad or success story to come out of America, or Korea, or the church down the road.

Pastors: *Love your people!* Enjoy their company. Listen to their stories. God has given them to you – and you to them. Everything God needs for His church at this moment He's provided! Maybe you'd like other things – another musician, a treasurer, a children's worker etc? They're things you'd like, but everything God requires He's provided. So trust Him and give thanks! Giving thanks is hugely important! Prayer and praising is a command so obey!

Everyone has their own way of belonging and committing, they may not be your ideas or your ways, but respect them. Folk must be loved where they are and how they are. Don't be concerned about the latest music or technology, God wants to capture our hearts! I'm constantly amazed that in spite of the fact that we use books (we don't even have an overhead projector), and don't have a clue about the newest songs etc. God's saving young and old without a projector or band in sight!

Preach love, mercy, grace, forgiveness, hope and acceptance. People don't need to hear how bad and messed up their lives are, they don't need you to tell them what they already know! They don't need another guilt trip, they need to know that the "somewhere over the rainbow" dream's come true! ". . . God has put eternity in the hearts of men . . ." (Ecclesiastes 3v11).

Bottom line – if you're serious about God's Kingdom: forget programmes; forget about plans "to bring people in". Stop seeing folk as "fodder for the Kingdom". It's not a competition! It's not a race! It's not about success and it's not about failure. It's not about growing or even trying to grow. Stop worrying and start loving!

Quite simply it's about following Jesus – together.

CHAPTER FIVE

VISION AND LEADERSHIP OF A SMALL CHURCH

Vision

> Vision is essential for survival – it is spawned by faith, sustained by hope, sparked by imagination and strengthened by God's Word. It is greater than sight, deeper than a dream, broader than an idea. It encompasses things outside the realm of the predictable, the safe and the expected. (Bob Gass, *Word for Today*)

God has a vision for every church and if His people seek His will, then by the power of the Holy Spirit, that vision will be achieved. Each church is there to reach out to those who don't yet know Christ and bring them into a loving family environment where each person is valued and grows. However, because each church is different, each will have a different way of fulfilling this vision in their location.

A *purpose* or *mission* is the "why we are here and what we should be doing" as a church.

A *vision* is what we have faith to believe that God will bring about if we fulfil our purpose. It's about having faith in what God will achieve rather than what we will manage to do.

In Proverbs it says: "where there is no vision, the people perish" (Proverbs 29v18 KJV).

A church without a vision is like a bus without a number or destination on the front. We want people to get on our bus, but they will rightly ask where we are going. "We don't know, just enjoy the ride!" won't keep them with us for long, even if they get on in the first place. It is important to seek God together for this direction for your church. This will give a sense of ownership and a purpose for all the activity. The overall purpose of any church is to make disciples, baptise them and teach them (Matthew 28v20), but God usually gives a way to bring this about in your locality with the people you have. Doing what God wants you to do honours Him and keeps the church in step with the Spirit.

Once God gives a vision, it needs to be caught by the whole church. It needs to be written down in a way that is understood by all. When the direction in which the church is going is established, everything that is done from preaching to community activities must be in line with that direction. It will help to have a short catchy version of the vision, which is published everywhere so people know it and can quote it when asked by visitors. Put it on banners or bookmarks, pencils or pens, calendars or newsletters and the church letterhead and website.

Examples of Small Church Vision Statements

Ashford Common Baptist Church

Vision

- Honouring God.
- Making disciples.
- Serving community.

The Leadership Team reviews this on an annual basis. Each year there is a Scripture verse or two taken as a motto to focus teaching and activities, publicised usually on banners, bookmarks and the monthly diary, all in line with the long term vision.

Canonbury Community Baptist Church

Aim

To build worshipping communities in Canonbury, west and east of Essex Road.

Objective

To reach widows and orphans. "Religion that God our Father accepts as pure and faultless is to look after orphans and widows in their distress and to keep oneself from being polluted by the world" (James 1v27 NIV).

Strategy

1. Build relationships with the community – "As he sent me I sent you."
2. Share a verbal witness – "Always be ready to make a defence to everyone who asks."
3. Invite community member to church/event – "How can they call unless they hear, how can they hear without a preacher?"
4. To incorporate the individual in to the fellowship – "They devoted themselves to the Apostles teaching and prayers."

5. Encourage and enable them to be part of a small group – "By this will all people know that you are my disciples if you show love for one another."
6. Encourage and enable each person to be part of the work of the church – "So in Christ, we who are many form one body."
7. Encourage and enable each person to be good users of their finances – "See to it that you excel in the grace of giving."

Leading a Small Church

What is a Leader?

> The common denominator of all growing churches is leadership that is not afraid to believe God. "According to your faith, will it be done to you" (Matthew 9v29 NIV). God uses the leader who has a dream, is willing to risk failure, expects the church to grow and who never gives up. (Ken Hyde, Broadmead Baptist Church)

In the New Testament, there are three main words in Greek with reference to those who lead in the churches:

Episkopos – overseer: a manager of people and able to see the big picture.
Poimen – shepherd or pastor: able to guide, care, lead.
Presbuteros – elder: an older person who has learnt by experience how to put faith into practice.

All three of these words come together in Acts 20v17–28 when Paul is issuing his last instructions to the leaders from Ephesus, describing them as elders, overseers and shepherds.

Ministers/pastors/leaders must be called to the task of leading a church – a "burning bush" or "milestone" moment, when God said

"This is what I want you to do for me". There will be tough days when the question "What am I doing here?" is asked, and at that point, they need to go back to that milestone and know again that God called them to that place at that time, and hasn't called them to move on yet.

Those who lead smaller churches are both men and women, although it is interesting to note that in the Baptist family 80% of women pastors are working in churches with 40 members or fewer. Peter quoted the prophet Joel at the fulfilment of the prophecy at Pentecost:

> In the last days, God says, I will pour out my Spirit on all people. Your sons and daughters will prophesy, your young men will see visions, your old men will dream dreams. Even on my servants, both men and women, I will pour out my Spirit in those days, and they will prophesy. (Acts 2v16–18 NIV)

Leadership can operate on a variety of levels determined by the time and resources available, but to see a group of God's people develop in their faith and reaching out in service to the local community is a rewarding job at every level.

Leadership Qualities

Paul outlined to Timothy the qualities required of overseers needed in Ephesus in his first letter:

> Now the overseer must be above reproach, the husband of but one wife, temperate, self-controlled, respectable, hospitable, able to teach, not given to drunkenness, not violent but gentle, not quarrelsome, not a lover of money. He must manage his own family well and see that his children obey him with proper respect. (If anyone does not know how to manage his own family, how can he take care of God's church?) He must not be a recent convert, or he may become conceited and fall under the same judgement as the devil. He must also have a good reputation with outsiders, so that he will not fall into disgrace and into the devil's trap. (1 Timothy 3v5–7 NIV)

We also look for qualities in church leaders not mentioned here by Paul such as:

- Be devoted to God – Father, Son and Holy Spirit.
- Be called and gifted by God to lead and able to lead, inspire and motivate.
- Have a willingness and genuine desire of heart to lead God's people.
- Lead by example of faith, prayer, demonstrate a servant heart.
- Be committed to teamworking and be accountable to other team members.
- Be prepared to delegate to and train others – don't be a control freak!
- Be aware of limitations – (you are not Superman or Wonder Woman!)
- Be open to challenges and changes.
- To enable people to know who they are in Christ, what their gifts are and provide opportunities for their use with helpful feedback (read Ephesians 1).

It is unrealistic to expect all these qualities or gifts in one person, so having a Leadership Team is a good solution for both the main leader/pastor/minister and the church as a whole.

Working as a Team

Working as a Leadership Team in a church reflects the Trinity who operate seamlessly together, Father, Son and Holy Spirit. Leadership when referred to in the New Testament is always plural, such as in Acts 15, 1 Peter 5v1 or this quote from Titus, "The reason I left you in Crete was that you might straighten out what was left unfinished and appoint elders in every town, as I directed you" (Titus 1v5 NIV).

Successes and failures can be shared rather than the praise or blame being on one person. There is always more creativity in a team, strengths are maximised, and life and faith experience is pooled. A team can possess many gifts between them so responsibilities can be given to suit the gifting. Communication is vital and it helps to know each other well, so spending time together outside the church setting is important.

Leadership awaydays are helpful. Aim to spend time as a team together at least once a year to pray, reflect, discuss and seek God for the way ahead. Good relationships build a better team. A leadership team will usually contain a main leader, a secretary, a treasurer and other leaders. In small churches, it is often the case that several of these offices are held by one person. A team ministry also ensures that if the main leader is ill or has personal issues to deal with, they can have time off and the church keeps going. Jobs can be rearranged and life goes on without applying extra pressure to an already difficult situation.

Conflict is perhaps inevitable in any group of people but good communication and an understanding of how each other ticks, will keep this to a minimum (see the Guideline to Resolving Conflict in the Tools section).

Team Working: The Flying "V"

When you see geese heading south for the winter flying along in V formation, you might consider what science has discovered as to why they fly that way. As each bird flaps its wings, it creates uplift for the bird immediately following. By flying in V formation, the whole flock has at least 71% greater flying range than if each bird flew on its own.

People who share a common direction and sense of common purpose can get where they are going more quickly and easily because they are travelling on the thrust of one another.

When a goose flies out of formation, it suddenly feels that drag and resistance of trying to go it alone and quickly gets back into formation to take advantage of the lifting power of the bird in front.

It is harder to do something alone than together.

When the lead goose gets tired, it rotates back into the formation, and another goose flies point at the head.

It is sensible to take turns doing demanding jobs. Shared leadership and interdependence give us each a chance to lead as well as opportunities to rest.

The geese in formation honk from behind to encourage those up front to keep up their speed.

What do we say when we honk from behind? We need to make sure our honking is encouraging and not discouraging.

Finally, and this is important, when a goose gets sick or wounded and falls out of formation, two other geese will fall out with that goose and follow it down to lend help and protection. They stay with the fallen goose until it is able to fly or it dies, and only then do they launch out on their own, or with another formation to catch up with their flock.

If we have the sense of a goose, we will stand by our colleagues and each other in difficult times as well as in good.

(Written by Angeles Arrien)

Leadership by Default!

Some small churches can afford, perhaps with grant assistance, to have a paid minister. However, in some small churches, the minister leaves and the Secretary and Deacons find themselves in charge. At those times they need, more than ever, the prayers of the fellowship. It is important for those leaders who didn't plan to be in sole charge to be assured that they are called by God and can be used by Him.

> Whatever you do, work at it with all your heart, as working for the Lord, not for men, since you know that you will receive an inheritance from the Lord as a reward. It is the Lord Christ you are serving. (Colossians 3v23–24 NIV)

This is a good time to take advice from those who have been in the situation before and appoint a Moderator or Association Consultant to work alongside the church, to assess where the church is spiritually and financially and to discuss the way forward. In these times, linking with other churches or support networks is vital, as described in the clusters and partnerships chapter.

Support and Prayers for the Leaders

> Churches get the leaders they pray for. (Martin Taylor, Ashford Common Baptist Church)

Church leaders can only fulfil their calling if supported and constantly lifted up in prayer by the other members of the fellowship. It is no bad thing for people within the church both to ask the leaders what they should be praying for and from time to time, tell them that they are praying in support of them and their work. Don't forget to also pray for their spouses and children as the pressures of ministry can be draining and costly. Ministers should be encouraged to take a sabbatical (3 months off) every seven years, usually a mixture of holiday, travel and study.

Leadership Training

In the Bible there are many examples of great leaders of men under God's instruction; Moses, Joshua, Gideon and David are a few examples. All inspirational role models and each varying in style, but for the perfect servant leader, look at Jesus himself. Rather than leading a mighty army, we see him choosing and calling twelve men and training them. He treats each one as an individual, developing their faith in Him and confidence in themselves. He models leadership for them in many ways, from washing their feet to demonstrating His power and authority over nature, sickness and Satan. He then gives them the power and authority required to go and do the same. He sends out the 12 disciples first, and after that successful mission, trains more men and sends out 72 the next time, again with amazing results (see Luke 10).

All good leaders train the next generation, mentoring people who God has called and gifted. Joshua was mentored by Moses, working alongside him, listening to his wisdom, and witnessing his close relationship with God. Jesus mentored his disciples, ensuring they had all they would need for the life of challenge ahead. Who are you training?

In a small church, you may look around the congregation and not see potential leaders. Pray that God would show you His thoughts on this, and if He shows you someone, be bold enough to take risks with them. Don't be put off if the person God seems to be directing you to is young. David was but a boy when he was called and anointed for service. It could be that your prayer has to be for a new person to come from outside to fill the role. As well as the full or part-time College courses to gain a formal qualification and accreditation, there are also local courses for Lay Pastors and Lay Preachers available in your area. However, these courses cannot fully equip someone for every eventuality. On the job training is as valuable as the formal training. It is important to keep fresh and attending conferences and other training opportunities that will input to your ministry and refresh you. There are many good books available to encourage you in your leadership role such as *The Leadership of Jesus* by Campbell McAlpine and *Courageous Leadership* by Bill Hybels.

Relationships in a Small Church

One minister said: "Having moved from my job in Africa, with the whole continent as my 'patch' and travelling to 42 out of the 51 countries there, co-ordinating a staff of over 300 and with a sizeable budget, it was not easy to adapt to a local church with a main morning congregation of 23! And yet I learnt an important lesson. Within a few short weeks, I

135

> discovered I was having contact at depth with more people, with more purpose, than in the years of glamorous evangelical jet-setting. I realised that God is not in the thunder, earthquake or mighty wind, but in the still, small voice. Small can be beautiful. Zechariah 4v6 says 'Not by might, nor by power but by My Spirit, says the Lord.'"[1]

The relationships built in a church are key to a minister's enjoyment of the job. Everyone will be happy to commit and work hard in a friendly, relaxed environment. In a small church, the relationships are more intense so friendships can be forged forever with some people, while others are sidelined.

Exercise Caution

The pastoral team of the church is often told very personal information during a one-to-one conversation, which of course is confidential (unless it is a matter for the Police or Social Services). This proviso must be made clear at the outset or divulging information to the authorities can be seen as betrayal. If there is a leadership team, people in the church can choose who they speak to about a problem, so it is right and helpful to have both men and women on the team. Care needs to be exercised with confidentiality during group prayer as it is all too easy to let out a confidence as a prayer request.

A leader must be careful when visiting people on a one-to-one basis, especially with the opposite sex. If the person to be visited is relatively unknown to you, vulnerable or unstable, always visit in pairs. (Remember what happened to Joseph in Genesis 39v6–20) There have been many cases where leaders have been inappropriately approached, and on their refusal to comply, have been slandered and falsely accused to the point of forcing them to leave the

---

[1] Stephen Gaukroger and David Cohen, *How to close your church in a decade* – used by permission.

ministry. Equally, we are all human and temptation can sometimes be hard to resist. It is wise for a married leader to tell their spouse who they will be visiting, especially if it is a member of the opposite sex.

If you are uncomfortable about praying "off the cuff" prayers with people when visiting them, there is nothing wrong with finding useful prayers in books to suit the occasion (sick, bereaved, troubled etc.).

Listening

It is recommended that a leader coming to a new situation should listen carefully to the congregation without making changes for the first few months. Listen and learn the church history from the long-standing key members, and retell it to build up faith. Looking back can often give a good platform from which to launch into the future. Because the members have been involved in looking back, they may be encouraged to look forward and even initiate some changes, not resist them as is likely with any fait accompli.

How to keep going

> It is difficult to have healthy, vibrant churches without healthy, vibrant leaders.

How do we achieve this? Spending quality time with God is essential to any ministry and following the example of Jesus, we need to be alone with the Father on a regular basis. We need to be in His presence, to just "be" and seek His face and sit at His feet. These are times of refreshing which strengthen us to carry on. As you are in your private devotion, be in your public devotion so people can see the love you have for Jesus.

Be aggressive towards your personal sin, not letting it take hold and become a habit, or breed bitterness. Confess it to God as soon as possible and receive His forgiveness. Paul also advised the

Ephesians: "Do not let the sun go down while you are still angry, and do not give the devil a foothold" (Ephesians 4v26–27 NIV).

It is important to have outside input into your ministry, a mentor or trusted friend who can offer a different perspective on issues and situations. Your Regional or Local Team will have a access to people who can help or advise on a wide variety of situations.

Keep a day a week to do something totally different to church work. Going out away from the phone and computer is recommended. Pursuing a hobby or sport, or enjoying family time help to recharge the batteries!

There will be times of rejoicing and tears, of joy and frustration, as is reflected in the Psalms. Leaders need God's wisdom in every area of ministry, knowing what to do and what to say, when to do nothing and when to be silent in any given situation. Following Paul's recommendations to the Thessalonians will keep your ministry on track.

> Live in peace with each other. And we urge you, brothers, warn those who are idle, encourage the timid, help the weak, be patient with everyone. Make sure that nobody pays back wrong for wrong, but always try to be kind to each other and to everyone else. Be joyful always; pray continually; give thanks in all circumstances, for this is God's will for you in Christ Jesus. Do not put out the Spirit's fire; do not treat prophecies with contempt. Test everything. Hold on to the good. Avoid every kind of evil.
>
> May God himself, the God of peace, sanctify you through and through. May your whole spirit, soul and body be kept blameless at the coming of our Lord Jesus Christ. The one who calls you is faithful and he will do it. (1 Thessalonians 5v13–24 NIV)

Pastoring a Small Church by Stuart MacKay, Lay Pastor at Broadclyst Baptist Church, Devon

I breathed a quick "Thank you Lord" as the music group finished playing and the stewards returned with the offering bags following the special collection for a new photocopier, scanner and page collator that we had just purchased. Each of the 270 folk present would have given generously and without doubt we wouldn't have to look at either "reserve funds" or "unbudgeted outgoings" in order to cover the cost. The fantasy disappeared as quickly as the morning mist and I truthfully looked out at the 16 wonderful people whom the Lord had entrusted to me . . .

Being Pastor of a smaller fellowship does have its own interests and areas of delight but there are times when it's difficult not to be disheartened and look negatively toward the future. The reality is that it is difficult with so many financial restraints, and, without being ageist, the lack of younger folk to share some of the work. It is perhaps as an indication of our fellowship that Sarah, my wife, who is an Assistant Head Teacher and I are the only people in the church who have a computer! Indeed at 57 I'm seen as one of the younger members!

Sadly some churches, such as ours, have for one reason or another not grown for many years and as the more elderly reach a time where they're either too old to come to church on Sundays or "go the way of all flesh", then not only do the numbers decrease but their spiritual gifts are also lost. So how do we start to overcome these and other problems?

A little while ago I was at a meeting when a friend came out with the comment, "God wants His church back!" and I was silent for a while as the truth of his words spoke to me. It made me realise that we, and perhaps other churches, (especially those who feel themselves under pressure) had lost our focus and to quote from Revelation 2v4 "had forsaken our first love". Maybe not consciously, but we certainly enjoyed, and I believe still do enjoy, our own little "safety zone" where we can trot along to church on a Sunday, feel a warm glow inside as we worship, meet with non-threatening people in a non-threatening situation and sing lovely songs that we knew as children. So the long haul starts as we go back to basics and pray that folks will be willing to get to know afresh who God really is, to give themselves totally to him and become eager and willing to become his disciples.

However, whilst all this is happening and we become a place to where people are drawn, it's also time for the pastor to spend time with the Lord and not only hear but obey what he says, and what's better than getting back to Scripture?

I've always regarded people's final words in a situation to be most important and Paul certainly didn't mince his words when he said goodbye to the Ephesian elders, but more important surely are the last words that Jesus said before ascending into heaven which must have a significant effect on each one of us. Just as a quick reminder Matthew 18:19 tells us "Therefore go and make disciples . . .". Does that mean then I need to do more than sit and pray that folks are going to pour into the church and if so then what? I suppose that there are several age groups that we can look at but with due respect to my dear fellowship, would it not be more advantageous to try to contact younger folk? But again that would mean having to bring them into a fellowship which would seem at least initially to be a meeting of the local 'Sunshine Club' and wouldn't really be culturally acceptable. What to do – what to do?

There was one group of people however that I just knew wasn't my gifting to reach and soon after I was inducted in January 2002, I told the Lord that I was happy to make contact and work with the local sixth-form students but forget about the rest because "I don't do kids!" After a little persistent nagging from the Lord, I wrote to the Head Teacher of the local Primary school and wasn't unduly unhappy when he told me that they weren't a Faith School and as far as he was concerned he didn't want any undue religious stuff in there. As can be imagined it was with some trepidation that I started sharing assemblies with the local Vicar by each of us presenting an assembly once a month. However man's ways aren't the Lord's ways and for various reasons I started becoming a more frequent visitor. Since then the Lord has moved in ways that only He can and in November 2004, the leader of the local Pre-school stopped me in the playground and said that whilst she wasn't a Christian and didn't believe in all that stuff, would I please drop in and tell the children the reality of Christmas? I soon found that during 2005 I was also visiting and presenting regular assemblies in the Pre-school. The Lord really does have a sense of humour ("I don't do kids") and as from the beginning of 2006, my time was spent apart from being the Pastor of the local Baptist Church, being once a week at Pre-school, four mornings a week doing assemblies with the Primary school and two lunch time clubs at the High School. During the middle part of 2006 I was asked and accepted the role of Trustee of the Pre-school and in December was asked if I would be Chaplain of the Primary School continuing on a more official basis my work not only with the students but also with parents, staff and governors.

We as a fellowship are excited at the doors that have been opened and give thanks that whilst there may be only a dozen to twenty in the "church building" on a Sunday morning, the church to who the Lord has called us to minister to also includes a "parish" of over 300 children and probably about 400 adults every week. I've now been asked to teach Christianity as part of the RE syllabus to Years 3–6, on a fortnightly basis. It's amazing what doors the Lord opens when we hand it all, including ourselves, over to Him.

I suppose that the reality is that if Jesus was prepared to go out into the community, which means reaching out with the love of God into a bewildered, sinful and hurting world and if we are going to be his true disciples, then we don't have much option but to follow him and do likewise – do we?

Yes, we do realise that it's going to be some time before we see what is perceived as being an abundant harvest, but at present the earth is being dug over and fertilised, seeds are being sown and watered and yes I do rejoice at every green shoot that starts to grow.

Our Minister is a Working Mum by Rev. Penny Marsh, Royal Docks Community Church, London

I am celebrating my eighth year at Royal Docks Community Church in Britannia Village, my first pastorate since graduating from London School of Theology.

Prior to full-time studies at college, I worked as Evangelist and Church Planter at Herne Hill Baptist Church. As part of my degree studies, I researched church plants on new housing developments and specifically in the Thames Gateway, London. This fuelled my interest and when I was invited to plant a church in Britannia Village, near London City Airport, I was thrilled.

The London Baptist Association sponsored me as a part-time pastor, which suited me as I'd just started a family. It was exciting to be part of a Christian presence right at the beginning of this new development. I started with just 3 people – myself, my husband and my son, and the support of another Baptist Church in Docklands.

I now work two-thirds time, which I fit around the children. As a working mum, I appreciate the flexi-hours, though it can be tricky, at times, to keep the right balance. Because there aren't many internal pastoral demands on my time I spend time visiting and networking outside the church and building relationships in the close knit community.

The 12 members are in their 30s–40s and 60s and a good balance of male and female, including a few people with special needs. I have two other people on my leadership team – a Scripture Union worker and my busy GP husband.

The church has an open attitude and a desire to connect with the community in as many ways as possible. Having started by delivering leaflets and running occasional events, they now have developed a community project with 2 staff members supported by secular funding.

The Bridges Community Project provides a number of services to people who may otherwise be isolated geographically, such as:

- Access to information and resources.
- Mum and Toddler group.
- Children's craft class.
- Monthly meeting for the elderly.
- Twice a week minibus trip for the elderly to the local supermarket, sponsored by a local hotel who provide both the minibus and the driver.

- Community drop-in.
- Links with Neighbourhood Watch and residents groups.
- Networking lunches for those who work with young people in the area.

The church has put on a variety of popular community events such as the Easter Egg Hunt (to which 199 children came), and local businesses (Tesco, Docklands Light Railway and the Thames Barrier Park) have been happy to sponsor them as part of their community involvement.

I am also the Chair of Governors at the local primary school, which my children attend and I've found that being a mum at the school gate is a great networking opportunity!

People are sometimes surprised to learn that I am the minister of the local church but the members are very happy to have a lady as pastor. I don't wear a collar so people get to know me before they know about my job.

Challenges

The main challenges I face are time-management and having an enormous mission but very few resources. The London Baptist Association is working on ways of helping me. I have good links with other local churches, however, many of these are also small. I am planning to explore the possibility of stronger links with some larger London Churches.

My prayer is that some of the many local contacts would discover Jesus for themselves, but in reality I see this as a long term goal.

Bi-vocational Ministry ("Tent-making") by Rev. S. Steve Gordon, Tasso Baptist Church, London

As a minister/evangelist, being bi-vocational has enabled me to work with a small central London church, where lack of people and financial resources has meant that only half a stipend could

143

initially be raised for its minister. I would say at the outset that being bi-vocational in practice is not a clear-cut equation of half time in secular work and half time in ministry; especially if you run a small business. The time pressures, duties and expectation to perform professionally and efficiently in both fields are very challenging. It is essential that if your work is one of self-employment that it is well thought out in regards to the support and resourcing that both your ministry and business will require e.g. expertise, personnel, administration and finance.

There is however the satisfaction of allowing an individual the opportunities to be part of and witness to a specific community/culture.

The Working Minister

The concept of the "working minister" has been one that was used extensively in the early stages of the developing Christian church, and today continues to be used for pioneering new ministries where a church needs to be replanted, or just where the local fellowship cannot afford a full-time fully paid minister.

Work – a Strategic Tool

The term we are used to hearing when speaking of Paul's ministry is tent-making. In Acts we read that following the martyrdom of Stephen, the believers were scattered and that as people settled they found new employment and working alongside their new neighbours, they gossiped the gospel and thus new churches began in Samaria, Antioch, and probably other cities (Acts 8v5; 11v19–21). Having a glorious message to proclaim affected those around these new believers. A bi-vocational / tent-making ministry itself can also be a way into a community and a witness to both the church and the community. To the church it speaks of a commitment and provides a means of keeping a Christian presence with a leader in situ where otherwise closure appears imminent.

As an electrician I now serve local businesses that are aware of my being a Christian and many opportunities for sharing the gospel present themselves. I continue to get to know the key figures in our community.

On one occasion a Bible was greeted with enthusiasm and gratitude from a widowed and retired HGV driver. Had I not been working alongside this man, I doubt very much whether that I would have had the same response.

Bridges are built when I work alongside local people as conversation flows with ease, and as they watch how I work, my values and attitudes hopefully speak volumes. Trust develops as we work, talk and laugh together and live in the same area. It is good to be recognised as I walk around the local streets being a part of the community, and people feel at ease when approaching me and more confident about coming into the church building.

Church Officers

Each church needs some structure and officers to fulfil the tasks of ministry. The right hand men and women of any pastor (full-time or part-time) are the officers, those committed people who give their time and talents to God as part of the team. Secretary, Treasurer and Deacon are posts that often sound onerous and complicated. This is not usually true especially in a small church where there are fewer people to look after and co-ordinate. There is always the possibility of taking a "divide and conquer" approach. The key then becomes putting an appropriately descriptive label to a subset of tasks and persuading a suitable person to take it on.

Church Secretary

In a traditional Baptist Church, the Church Secretary was the acknowledged leader of the diaconate/eldership, a gifted administrator in the broadest sense who naturally dealt with the minister on behalf of the church and the person to whom the whole church turned when the minister moved on. In a small church, because lack of numbers usually means lack of gifted volunteers, that role can be impossible to fill. However, there are no legal requirements for this particular role to exist. There may be Church rules to abide by, but even these are unlikely to give a detailed job description, so tune the job to fit the situation.

Useful resources for all Church Secretaries and Administrators:

Nothing Spiritual About Chaos book by Rachel Tole (Baptist Union Publications). See Baptist Union Guidelines at www. baptist.org.uk, or phone 01235 517700 for a paper copy.

Church Treasurer

In a medium or large church there will probably be several people willing and able to take on all the tasks associated with the Treasurer role and also be capable of acting as part of the leadership team at the same time. In a small church, it is often necessary to split tasks because no one person has all the necessary skills.

The Leadership Team (Elders/Deacons/Trustees/Directors) are accountable for the financial dealings of the Church. They are accountable to God, to the Church, and also in law, to the Charity Commission. In addition to requirements that brings on who may act as a leader (or more strictly as a Trustee), it brings requirements on what they must do as a team. Thus at the very least they must oversee all the financial processes including Strategy (where will we accept money from, where will we spend it), Tactics (in particular the budget for the year) and Governance.

With all financial governance, there are 4 key tools that are employed to protect the innocent and reduce the risk of loss. These are:

1. Written records.
2. Separation of duties.
3. Rotation of duties.
4. Audit.

It is good practice for the process of counting cash to have two people involved, and for them to record the result. It is good practice to have two signatures required on cheques and never to allow a signature on a blank cheque. It is good practice to give your bookkeeper a sabbatical. It is good practice (and a charity requirement) to have the accounts independently reviewed annually.

It is best practice to document the various processes, and then ensure the processes are followed. The tasks of bookkeeping, tending bank accounts, preparing financial reports, paying salaries and handling cash can all be delegated to trusted individuals or bodies, not necessarily the Treasurer.

It is poor practice for the main leader of a church to act in addition as the treasurer or bookkeeper or cashier. It breaks the separation of duties rule, and may make it easier for the others to be overlooked.

Help is available from some Regional Teams in the form of a payroll system for Church Treasurers where the numbers are "crunched" and the amounts payable to pensions/minister/PAYE etc. are then sent back to the Treasurer who simply writes the cheques.

Useful resources for Church Treasurers: Baptist Union Guidelines at www.baptist.org.uk or phone 01235 517700 for a paper copy.

Church Deacon

The word "deacon" comes from the Greek word *Diakonos* which means servant. This first appears in Acts chapter 6 where men who were full of the Spirit and wisdom were chosen to deal with the more practical aspects of the new church while the Apostles concentrated on prayer and the ministry of the word. "Deacons, likewise, are to be men worthy of respect, sincere, not indulging in much wine, and not pursuing dishonest gain. They must keep hold of the deep truths of the faith with a clear conscience" (1 Timothy 3v8–9 NIV). In a small church the deacons (or leadership team) find themselves with many and varied tasks in order to support the minister, and in times of interregnum lead the church forward. There are different ways to elect deacons, but usually the church meeting recognises the gifts and talents as well as the serving attitude in the nominees and vote to support them in their new posts. Deacons, along with the minister and other officers are often the trustees of the church so must be aware of the responsibility before accepting such a post. It is often hard to find people in a small church who are willing to stand as deacons, but if the essential tasks can be divided up, the task is not so onerous.

What's involved in being a Church Secretary? by Peter Osbourne, Secretary of Yiewsley Baptist Church, Middlesex

Prior to considering whether to allow myself to be nominated for Secretary of our Church, I asked the outgoing Secretary if he would list the responsibilities of the role, which he did as follows:

General
1. Ability to work with and support the Pastor 100%.
2. Deal with correspondence concerning all Church matters.
3. Deal with any matters concerning the Church buildings and Manse.
4. Preparation, after agreement with the Pastor, and distribution before the meeting, of Agendas for Deacons and Church members meetings.
5. Produce the meetings minutes and arrange distribution.
6. Maintain stock of paper and toner for photocopier.
7. Maintain supply of Communion wine.
8. Maintain Church Members register.
9. Keep Church notice board up to date.
10. Prepare Vestry Prayer and Communion rosters.

Annually
1. Prepare and supply statistical information for Baptist Union and Association as required.
2. Agree with Pastor his 5 weeks annual leave and 4 additional Sundays off.
3. Ensure that speakers are booked well in advance for the services of these 9 Sundays. Ensure that they are fully briefed e.g.

time of service, children's talk in the morning service and whether a communion service is scheduled.

4. During the week prior to the engagement check with the speaker that he/she is still available and reconfirm arrangements. Obtain hymn numbers and pass to musicians prior to Sunday (this also serves as a reminder for the speaker!).

5. Arrange for the annual service for boilers.

Weekly

1. Set the boiler programme and be prepared to switch boilers on and off for additional events.

2. Prepare and announce notices.

3. Prepare communion and collect and wash glasses afterwards.

4. Ensure that fresh water is available for pastor/speaker at both services.

5. Open and close church building for services including checking general security of buildings.

Needs of a Secretary

A crystal ball and the ability to read the minds of all members, because you are rarely advised about what is happening, but nonetheless you are expected to know! It was not until I saw it listed out, that I realised the extent of the responsibilities of a Secretary and there were some that were not even there e.g. liaising with the various church and non-church organisations.

On the basis that many of the small churches will not have a Pastor, I will concentrate my comments on those points that would affect those churches. Can I firstly suggest that there is no need for one person to have to undertake all the above items? I made the point to our Church prior to the election that I would *not* be undertaking all the aspects highlighted in the list above, because I believed it would make it very difficult for one person to take over this role in the future. I also said I would make mistakes (and I certainly have!) but, as with all of us, I would be trying my best. I have found that has stifled criticism of minor issues that sometimes can, in a small church, become magnified out of context.

Shortly after my election I approached various members, some on the diaconate, some not and asked if they would take over some of these aspects e.g. Deacons to rotate in dealing with points 6,19 and 20. Two members took over point 3, and another member took over point 6. If you have a member who can take minutes then that is another gift which can be utilised. (We have also done the same thing with the Treasurership: one member counts the offering and takes it to bank, another looks after Gift Aid etc).

With regards to speakers, network with secretaries of other local churches to obtain more speakers names, utilise the London Baptist Association Preachers database if in the London Area (0208 977 1279) and do not forget other denominations as this can help to forge new relationships. Legislation is continuing to affect us all e.g. Fire regulations, so ensure that you take note of all the items in Transform (Info for Secretaries and Treasurer from the Baptist Union) or check the Baptist Union website for current issues.

Whilst all the above are very necessary for the smooth running of the Church, I believe a very important aspect is to keep a finger on the pulse of the church to pre-empt any issues which may, long term, cause difficulties if they are not identified at an early stage. I see one of my most important roles as being the oil between the wheels of the membership including ensuring that the quieter voices as well as the louder are represented in the life of the Church.

If issues are dealt with quickly, and often it is only a case of letting a voice be heard, then they will, generally, not cause long term problems. It is in a church united in prayer and praise of our Lord and serving its community that the Holy Spirit can really work in power and that can be the greatest work that the Church Secretary can help to achieve.

Finally, and especially for a church without a Pastor, the Secretary's job can be a lonely one. You will in reality be the head of that Church and it can be difficult, particularly if criticism is made of you, despite it perhaps being incorrect or unfair. Ask your Diaconate to support you and if at all possible, have them very much involved in visible leadership, so that members can be pointed to different people depending on the issue, rather than you having to carry the whole burden.

What was my biggest problem? The heating system! We had so many different events going on at random times that ensuring, whilst working full time, that it was always correctly on proved a challenge, and not surprisingly no one else wanted that task!

Despite this one aspect I feel I am serving the Lord in this most important role in the church.

What's involved in being a Church Treasurer? by Norman Smith, Treasurer of Ashford Common Baptist Church, Middlesex

I was always good at maths in school, being brought up with long multiplication and division using £.s.d and imperial measures. I have kept my feel for numbers and this has been useful when doing church accounts. I do not have a computer but the church leaders do and they feed my monthly figures into their spreadsheets for budgeting.

Integrity is vital as well as a clean criminal record in the financial department. Money laundering and other checks are made every time an account is opened or a new signatory added, so it would be embarrassing for the Church Treasurer to fail.

Charity Law

See also the Charities, Trustees and Trusteeships section in Chapter 9.

At the time of writing, churches do not have to register with the Charity Commissioners but have "Excepted Charity" status. It has been rumoured for many years that this is about to change. However, Charity Law has to be followed. For small churches, the payments and receipts procedure must be followed. For turnover less than £100,000 no independent examination is necessary. Above £100,000 the accruals type of bookkeeping is needed. This sum excludes expenditure of a capital nature such as buying or enlarging property. Maintenance and redecoration are not capital projects. Income and expenditure of all such funds must be included.

Bookkeeping

If using a paper based system, you need a book with at least 16 columns over two pages to cover the various types of expenditure. We use a double entry system where each transaction is entered both in a category and whether it was cash or cheque. We use a fresh page each month. At the month-end each column is totalled and the net profit or loss shown by each method (category, cash/cheque) should agree. We also calculate the cumulative since the start of the church year. There should also be agreement with the bank balance. We pay extra to have weekly statements for our current account as some people give by standing order and some bills are paid by direct debit. The advantage of a book is that it is portable and can be taken to church meetings so any questions can be readily answered. It is also somewhere for the Independent Examiner to sign.

Sub-funds

These include items such as the expenses of keeping a pastor. We also have a Partnership Fund to support a church in India. Various groups such as Sunday school may also run their own (sub) accounts. Another feature is Designated and Restricted Funds. Totals of transactions from sub-accounts/funds must be fed back into the main account.

Taxation

Her Majesty's Revenue and Customs (HMRC) want their money! This is for National Insurance (employee and employer) and Income Tax for every paid employee. Dispensations are available for books and telephone and there are special arrangements with regard to paying manse fuel bills. If the payments to HMRC are fairly small (less than £1,500 per month) they may be done quarterly by agreement. There is 2 weeks allowed to get them in.

The Financial Intermediaries and Claims Office (FICO) run the Gift Aid Scheme, which allows the church to reclaim tax on donations. The work involved includes getting declaration forms signed and donations identified and recorded. The claims procedure is relatively straightforward once they have cleared the Treasurer regarding honesty. They are willing to pay the money into the church bank account using BACS Direct Credit.

Insurance

Public and employer insurance are needed, the latter because volunteers are classed as unpaid employees. It is worth considering whether specific items should also be covered such as office equipment and musical instruments. Of course buildings and contents should be included if appropriate.

Data Protection Register

If you keep records that can identify a person – e.g. who has set up a Gift Aid regular payment – you will need to consider whether it needs to be covered under a registration. Confidentiality should be respected. Consult your Regional Team for detail advice.

Records

Receipts should be obtained for payments made, either from the recipient or authority to pay from one of the church officers. I keep records for the traditional 6 years. Employer Insurance Certificates have to be retained for 40 years.

Finally . . .

This all may sound terrifying but it is not too onerous once you get into it. If starting from scratch, then visit the Treasurer of a nearby church of a similar size to see how they work. The Baptist Union have leaflets and guidelines on various topics and updates are published in *Transform* and on the web (www.baptist.org.uk). The Baptist Insurance Company Ltd enrol their clients' treasurers in The Association of Church Accountants and Treasurers who provide a thick loose-leafed book of information.

What's involved in being a Church Deacon? by Jan Williams, Deacon at Haddenham-cum-Dinton Baptist Church

Working alongside the Minister, there are 6 deacons at Haddenham-cum-Dinton Baptist Church and we each take responsibility for our areas of gifting, as seen below:

Ron – Auditor, communion convenor, technical (audio) co-ordinator, looking after the burial ground.

David – Secretarial support, Churches Together in Haddenham representative.

Sheila – Pastoral care co-ordinator, Christian aid committee, flower distribution, "Carols" (a chatroom for young people), children's advocate.

Jane – Secretary and pianist/organist.

Jan – Mission team, BMS representative, flower secretary, transport co-ordinator.

Paul – Treasurer, Crafty kids club.

On the list of church officers, we plus 24 others are named as having areas of service to the church and community. Mobilising the whole small church to action is no mean feat, but that is what we have done in this church of 30 members. Each feels a part of the church and we all pull together as a team to impact the community for God.

Each Sunday, the Deacons are on a duty rota and the tasks are:

- Opening/closing premises.
- Delivering notices.

- Glass of water in pulpit and porch.
- Counting attendees.
- Check hymn numbers.
- Distribute news letters.
- Bring children from Sunday School into church.
- Act as Fire Officer.
- Place traffic cone outside.
- Check lights/heating and audio systems on/off.

For me personally, becoming a Deacon was and is a very humbling and sometimes overwhelming experience. Having the life of the church at one's fingertips is a real privilege and to be able to serve the church and take God's love out in to the community must be uppermost in the Deacons duties. One becomes a "bodyguard" to the minister – encouraging, supporting and making sure they have the proper time off. Being a Deacon means serving in the life of the church and for me the very essence of this is praying and serving at Holy Communion.

Ron Buttery writes . . .

For me, being a deacon can be easily summarised in a single word – service. It is not necessary to have an encyclopaedic knowledge of the Bible or be an expert in theology or be well versed in church and inter-denominational politics . . . all that is required is a genuine willingness to serve others and to have an unshakeable faith in the risen Christ. Being chosen as a deacon by your fellow Christians is an honour and in its own way a sort of calling that gives you the opportunity to be of even greater service to the Lord than simply being a church member.

LEADERSHIP TOOLS

Reflections for Church Leaders

These questions are designed for personal reflection for the Leadership in the church, potentially leading to a discussion of the answers.

- Do you know your primary gifting?
- Do you feel able to delegate the jobs you are not good at?
- Who is part of the Leadership team? Secretary, Treasurer, Deacons
- How can any vacant posts be filled?
- Do you work together as a team?
- How could this relationship be improved?
- Do you meet together socially?
- Do you have 'awaydays' to seek God's will and direction for the church?
- Does the church have a vision?
- Have you a mentor or friend who can encourage you during the tough times?
- Do you meet with other church leaders locally for mutual support?
- Do you go on regular conferences, training courses or other sources of input?
- Do you encourage people in your church to go on training courses to suit their gifting e.g. Children's ministry, youth ministry, treasurers training etc
- How are the relationships in your church? Does it have a family feel, or is it a group of individuals who meet together?
- Are there opportunities for the church to meet socially together outside meetings?
- How do you put across God's truth in a way that people enjoy and remember?

One final thought – when all else fails, keep your sense of humour.

Small Group Activity

This activity enables people to dream or to reveal their dreams in a group. The results may surprise you.

On a sheet of paper, ask each person to write down the answers to these two questions:

1. What would you attempt for God if you had the resources and knew you couldn't fail?
2. What would be the first steps you would take to reach that goal?

Share the results together.

Purpose

Every church exists for a reason, but most churches do not consider their purpose.

Exercise – encourage every church member to pray and then complete this sentence: "*This church exists in order to . . .*".

Weigh the answers and reach a consensus.

Hone it into one sentence that all are happy with.

Once the purpose is agreed, major objectives need to be set for key areas like:

- Worship.
- Pastoral care.
- Evangelism.
- Discipleship.
- Service.

Now, short term objectives or goals need to be set. They need to be S. M. A. R. T:

- Specific – means that your goal is to the point.
- Measurable – means that you will know when you have reached your goal.
- Achievable – means that your goal is something you are expecting to achieve.
- Relevant – means that your goal is right for you at this time and you will benefit from achieving it.
- Time-framed – means that you set yourself a time limit to achieve it in which is realistic.

It is important to celebrate each achievement as this lifts spirits and increases motivation.

Guidelines For Resolving Conflict

Rule of Thumb: No matter who started it, I have the responsibility to take the initiative to seek reconciliation – either by offering forgiveness or apologising and asking for forgiveness. This remains true, no matter how embarrassing or awkward it may seem. When conflict exists, try following through the collection of Scriptures below.

Philippians 4v6–7 and Matthew 6v6	Pray before taking any action.
1 Peter 5v7 and Romans 8v28	Bring your negative feelings to God first. Thank Him for the good which He desires will come from the situation.
Acts 24v16 and Proverbs 28v13	Pursue a clear conscience and expect God to show mercy and blessing.
Matthew 5v23	Seek reconciliation with those who have something against you before carrying on with "worship as normal".

Matthew 5v24 and Philippians 2v2	Make loving reconciliation your goal, not proving you were right all along.
Titus 3v2 and Matthew 7v3–5	Before going, identify and confess your own wrong attitudes, asking God to give you His attitude and perspective.
Philippians 2v3 and James 2v4	Go with a humble spirit, not an air of moral superiority.
Philippians 2v4 and Mark 10v43–44	Try to see the matter from the other's perspective, to understand and serve their interest as much as possible.
2 Corinthians 6v3 and 1 Corinthians 8v9–13	Do not refuse to admit that part of the blame might be yours. Acknowledge your own failures in the matter.
Ephesians 4v15, 25, 29–32 and Proverbs 14v29	Describe your negative feelings honestly and kindly, without a bitter, accusing spirit, but also without lying to the one who offended you about how you really feel.
Romans 12v17–21 and 1 Peter 2v12	Incorporate an act of kindness to highlight your genuine desire for reconciliation.
James 5v16	Pray with the other party before ending the conversation.
1 Timothy 2v5 and Matthew 18v16	Consider the role that a neutral third party might play as mediator if the initial caring confrontation was fruitless.

CHAPTER SIX

CHILDREN AND YOUNG PEOPLE IN A SMALL CHURCH

Children – the most exciting people on the planet!

Children are one of the church's most valuable assets. They are also the most vulnerable, so your ministry with them is a vitally important one. (Margaret Withers, *Where two or three . . .* Church House, 2004)

Children have an amazing capacity for all things spiritual and watching them worship and use gifts of the Spirit moves us deeply.

> At that time Jesus said, "I praise you, Father, Lord of heaven and earth, because you have hidden these things from the wise and learned, and revealed them to little children." (Matthew 11v25 NIV)

> You will know that I am in Israel, that I am the LORD your God, and that there is no other; never again will my people be shamed. And afterwards, I will pour out my Spirit on all people. Your sons and daughters will prophesy, your old men will dream dreams, your young men will see visions. Even on my servants, both men and women, I will pour out my Spirit in those days. (Joel 2v27–32 NIV)

God Loves Children and Young People

We read in the Bible of children such as Isaac and Ishmael who God saved from certain death as He had a plan for their lives. Hannah had prayed so long for a son that she promised the child to God if her prayers were answered. When Samuel was born, he lived and worked at the temple. He learnt to discern the voice of God and was gifted as a prophet. He anointed David, a shepherd boy as king-to-be of Israel.

Jesus himself healed children and welcomed them to Him for a blessing.

> People were bringing little children to Jesus to have him touch them, but the disciples rebuked them. When Jesus saw this, he was indignant. He said to them, "Let the little children come to me, and do not hinder them, for the kingdom of God belongs to such as these. I tell you the truth, anyone who will not receive the kingdom of God like a little child will never enter it." And he took the children in his arms, put his hands on them and blessed them. (Mark 10v13–16 NIV)

Are we like Jesus welcoming children or are we like the disciples who thought they were a nuisance?

Children and Young People are an Integral Part of the Church Family

In both the Old and New Testaments, there are occasions where the whole company of God's people are called together to pray. An example of this is in Acts 21v2–6 when the church gathered to pray for Paul and his companions before they left Tyre.

> We landed at Tyre, where our ship was to unload its cargo. Finding the disciples there, we stayed with them seven days. Through the Spirit they urged Paul not to go on to Jerusalem. But when our time was up, we left and continued on our way. All the disciples and their wives and children accompanied us out of the city, and there on the beach we knelt to pray. (Acts 21v3–5 NIV)

Do we welcome children to our prayer meetings? Do we think they can reach the Father's heart and bring words from Him? Do we give them the opportunity?

In small churches particularly, each child can be known by name by the whole congregation. For church members' children, it can be invaluable to have other Christian adults to talk to apart from their parents. Children that arrive unaccompanied may enjoy having a group of all age people as new friends who can influence them for God, encourage them and spend time talking and answering questions. It is good for the children to have older people to chat to as they may not often see their grandparents. Because of the family feel that often prevails in smaller churches, children are readily accepted as part of the church, and hopefully fully involved.

Teaching the truth of Scripture to children is a directive from Deuteronomy.

> Love the LORD your God with all your heart and with all your soul and with all your strength. These commandments that I give you today are to be upon your hearts. Impress them on your children. Talk about them when you sit at home and when you walk along the road, when you lie down and when you get up. (Deuteronomy 6v5–7 NIV)

Simple Faith and Dependence on Our Father

> At that time the disciples came to Jesus and asked, "Who is the greatest in the kingdom of heaven?" He called a little child and had him stand among them. And he said: "I tell you the truth, unless you change and become like little children, you will never enter the kingdom of heaven. Therefore, whoever humbles himself like this child is the greatest in the kingdom of heaven." And whoever welcomes a little child like this in my name welcomes me. But if anyone causes one of these little ones who believe in me to sin, it would be better for him to have a large millstone hung around his neck and to be drowned in the depths of the sea. (Matthew 18v1–6 NIV)

We must heed the warning of Jesus not to lead children astray, but to welcome them as an integral part of the church family. At any age, people are welcomed into God's family and called His children. A Father and child relationship of love is what God longs to have with us, being dependent on Him for life itself and Him lavishing gifts on us.

Welcome and Love All Children and Young People

Children in our small churches can be not only diverse in age, but also diverse in life experience and faith. From those who have grown up in Christian homes (who often see themselves as Christians), to those who only know Jesus' name as a swear word, to those from different religious backgrounds. We must cater for them all because God loves each one of them.

As God's representatives on earth, we in the church are called to imitate His love and share the desire that all should be saved and none should perish. We are called to care for all people, especially the young and vulnerable.

Society has changed so much leaving a trail of destruction in its wake. Single parents try to juggle a job and bring up children single-handed, many children do not have a male role model in their formative years and some have suffered abuse and now do not trust anybody. Add to this the ever-changing cultural influences which bring their own challenges.

163

A Sobering Thought . . .

Who Loves Your Baby?

The church was finding it difficult to get enough people to help with the children's work.

"I'm sorry" some people said "We'd love to help, but we just don't have the time to go to all the planning sessions."

"That's all right" said the pornographic magazine vendor "I like children, I'm prepared to stay open all hours to give the children magazines to read."

The church still wanted some of its members to help.

"Sorry" they said "We need to spend time in worship and learning from the preaching for the adults."

"That's all right, I'll help" said the drug pusher, "I like spending my time talking and building relationships with the children."

The church still wanted some of its members to help.

"Sorry" they said "We're just no good with children."

"That's all right. I'll help" said the video producer. "I don't know anything about children, but I'll go on training courses and work late to find out all about young people so I can make the videos they want to watch. And when it comes to scenes of violence, I'll make sure I am on the right side of the law."

The church still wanted some of its members to help.

But it was the magazine vendor, the drug pusher and the video producer who worked the hardest at their children's work.

Anon

"Tweenagers"

This "new" group of children aged 9-to-13 years of age are caught in the middle of still being children and an increasingly teenage awareness of life. Companies in the fashion and technology industries are realising there is an emerging group of younger people who have a rising allowance and the freedom to spend it so are therefore aiming to cater for their every whim. Ideas on TV and in magazines which are designed for older teens are now appealing to this tweenage bracket. They have grown up with technology and about 50% of them own a mobile phone so they "chat" to their friends using text messages.

However, children are now more aware of national and global issues than before (thanks to TV) and are concerned about eating healthily, the state of the planet and wanting the world to be a better place. This age group has more independence and is more streetwise than the same age group just 10 years ago and often have to make decisions for themselves rather than being told what to do. They decide who to have respect for and feel that people have to earn it rather than automatically have it because they are an adult.

A good number of tweenagers enjoy being in church groups with their friends, and appreciate the rules and boundaries set for them. They are eager to find out about life and so regularly ask random questions on all subjects, to both genuinely enquire and to shock. They respond well to being given responsibility so that asking them one at a time to help the youth leaders to run a class or an evening will have many benefits.

In a small church especially, we have the opportunity for one to one or small group conversation where we can be supportive to the young people and their ever changing lives and issues that they face. The mixture of activities they enjoy varies greatly, but we may have to change our perception about what suits which age group.

Youth

1. Young people are people (not another species!). Approach young people as whole people, not just telling them that God

loves them (they don't know who God is, they don't know what love is and they don't know who they are).

2. Youth ministry is a Church issue (must not be thought of and treated as separate).
3. God is at work in youth ministry.

Five Common Misconceptions about Youth Work

1. You need big budgets and lots of resources to do youth ministry (no – youth ministry is all about relationships not programmes!).
2. You need a big, well equipped building to do youth work (no – it can be done anywhere).
3. You need people in their 20s and 30s to staff youth ministry (no – even grannies can have a youth ministry.
4. You need a critical mass to do youth ministry (no – all you need is one youth).
5. Every church needs youth work to ensure its future (no – the church future actually depends on doing mission, not specifically youth mission).

Lack of Numbers – positive and negative

If you only have one or two teenagers, be willing to introduce them to another fellowship where there are others, especially for social interaction. The teen years are a time when being part of a peer group is vital for growth and the establishment of individual identity. However, there is an opportunity for relationships to be built with young people in a small church, e.g. in a discussion group midweek (with food!) where low numbers are not an issue. Outings are also easier to organise if there is only a small group.

Sex, Drugs and Rock and Roll

Be willing for sexual matters to be discussed; gently correct errors of fact, don't be judgmental, and don't believe all they say or boast about. In Chapter 9 there is a resource for teaching teens what the

Bible says about sex. Teenage pregnancy is a major issue in the UK and many girls feel under pressure.

It is important for youth workers to go on awareness training about drugs and how to spot the symptoms of use. (Your local Community Police Officer will advise on courses run by the Police). With the young people, discuss smoking, drug taking and alcohol and why teens feel the need to escape from life using these temporary fixes. Except in extreme circumstances, do not repeat what is said to any parents. Have a clear church policy on how to deal with matters that you think should be referred to parents, Social Services or the Police. (The local secondary school may have such a policy that can be adapted for church use).

Make sure that you are aware of what is "hot" news for young people, including keeping up to date with the latest pop music and groups.

Listening

Be open to discuss any issue that a young person wants to talk about. Many teens think that there are few adults who have time to listen to them, so finding a listening ear in a church context is a good witness. It is important not to laugh or look shocked at what they may tell you as most of the time they will genuinely be looking for advice.

Youth Work in a Small Church by Moira Kleissner, now at Christ Church, Ipswich

A small church in Hammersmith, London had been running a children's club for several years, manned by the minister and two church members. They were then able to afford to share a Time For God volunteer with the local Salvation Army, so started up a youth club.

After that had been going for a couple of years, several of the children said they wanted a discussion and Bible study group. If the leaders had suggested it, it would probably have fallen flat, but as it came from them, the study group was established. The minister's wife took this on with the help of a mum and the Time For God volunteer.

There was a small room in the church that they used and the girls asked if they could decorate it. They ended up with red walls with large brightly coloured and silver geometric patterns, an orange door and purple skirting boards. Bring your sunglasses! They finished off the room with bean bags. The girls came shopping and helped to buy the stuff and did the painting. The group was called the Discovery Zone.

Over the next two years, they had between 12 girls and 5 boys each Wednesday night for one and a half hours. Materials were a problem as the age range was 10–14 years including some hyperactive kids, so no run around games. Youth Alpha was totally inappropriate, Rock Solid was too expensive for a small church, and nothing else could be found at that time, so the minister's wife got writing. She was able to produce, with the help of colleagues at CURBS (Children in Urban Situations) a pack called Zero to Hero (this has now been published and can be found on the website www.curbsproject.org.uk) and it is designed for 10–14s. When that course finished, they discovered Youth Emmaus which was exactly the kind of introduction and development on Christianity that was needed.

Discovery Zone has now folded as the children have gone onto studies or moved out of the area (The church is in an area of high population turnover, just half an hour from Heathrow Airport but with soaring house prices). We know that the discussions, Bible studies and cookery classes benefited those who came to the Discovery Zone, because the children themselves decorated the room and worked out their own discipline structure – RESPECT – they owned the group and it wasn't "us" and "them" but "us together". We also had great fun on trips once a term to the ice rink, 10 pin bowling, pizza restaurant and swimming.

Yes, small churches can do youth work, but it needs to be of God and with people who can communicate to this age group, having seriously thought through what the aims of the group will be before they start.

Zion Pentre: a Welsh Chapel that started a youth club by Rev. David Brownnutt, formerly Minister of the Rhondda Baptist Network

You don't need to be young to help in a youth club. Most of Zion's youth workers are over 70. Zion has 16 active members, mainly in their 70s. Three teenagers walked in one January to get out of the cold. They got such a good welcome that they came again.

The members went out of their way to make the youngsters welcome. For example, the first time I preached after they started coming, I announced my second hymn and one of the old ladies called out and told me I couldn't have that hymn as their young people wouldn't know it. The service was halted while the members discussed with their young people what hymns they would like. I was then given a revised hymn list.

After a month or so, the teenagers asked for a youth club. Fiona Michael (head of Youth For Christ Cymru) who lived a couple of villages away agreed to run it for the chapel on condition that they helped. Two members are present each time to welcome the children and do the refreshments, though they have been known to join in quieter games. The first volunteer to help was Beryl who is 91!

Fiona asked for a budget. Chapel cash-flow was a bit tight so she was given the old Sunday school account which was sitting doing nothing and the members also each gave £1 a week into the youth club fund. Fiona later suggested that they started giving less as the money was coming in faster than she could spend it!

The average youth club attendance is 6. In October we took 4 of them to Cardiff for the Youth Revival Celebrations in the Cardiff International Arena organised by Ignite. It was a great evening. The youngsters have now asked for a catering lesson so that they can throw a Christmas party for the old people who help run the youth club for them.

TOOLS FOR WORK WITH CHILDREN AND YOUNG PEOPLE

Questions

A list of questions to be considered by the Church.

Do we need to do Children's or Youth work?
This is the first question that a church needs to ask if there is any doubt. In some areas there may be very few children or a flourishing Sunday School at another church. Then your church may feel that it should concentrate on a different kind of ministry e.g. for older people, people with learning difficulties, people with mental health problems, people with alcohol or drugs problems. Each church needs to ask and seek God's leading for their specific ministry.

However if a church feels that God wants them to minister to children and teenagers, there may still be some problems. These, however, are not insurmountable, just work with what and who you have.

Have you a lack of children or youth but willing leaders?
Today we have many more disrupted families (alternate weekends with mum and dad), sports, dance classes and other activities on a Sunday. Set up a midweek club instead and use the available and relevant materials.

Do you lack leaders but have some children?
If you have some children but not many leaders, there are several solutions:

Look at all age material rather than breaking the children into age groups. "Godly Play" (website www.godlyplay.org.uk) is an excellent method of doing this using Bible stories.

Key Stage 1 children can have a short teaching period while the Key Stage 2 children do an activity in the same room, then reverse

170

it. This can be noisy so bear this in mind when preparing. If you have 2 teachers, one should do Key Stage 1 and the other do Key Stage 2. Teaching two groups in the same room keeps within the 'Safe to Grow' parameters of two adults present.

There are many good RE class or assembly materials available that can easily be used in a church context and will be suitable for small numbers.

Speak to an experienced Christian school teacher, as they can be a mine of information.

For resources, see Chapter 9.

Is the church Sunday service child friendly?
You might like to try a different kind of church experience like an all-age service, rather than children and young people being on the fringe or excluded. In this model the main church service is geared for everyone from 0–100 years old and uses a multi-sensory approach rather than a hymn, prayer, sermon sandwich. Because all ages are involved in seeing, hearing, touching and doing, they remember more and learning is more fun.

> Gaer Baptist Church has tried this as a 4pm Sunday family service followed by refreshments. They called it Time4God and was much enjoyed by all ages. They have used play-dough, pebbles, pipe cleaners, and post-it notes to illustrate the theme and guide prayer times. They also used stories with "actions" for the listeners to join in with. They found worship videos helpful (ones with scenery and music) using them on an ordinary TV screen which worked as numbers were small enough for this.

Is there a lack of space?
You may not need as much room as you think. Throw out all the junk and rubbish from the church building. Make an allocated room or corner of a room bright and attractive, and get the children

to help decorate it. One small church had the teenagers group meeting in the vestry, which they decorated completely with pop posters! If you use a corner of the church, use brightly coloured screens and bean bags and unusual lamps to make it special for the youngsters.

> A small church with just one large worship area in Llanrumney bought large dust sheets and painted them with cartoon characters, then hung them on string right round the room. They are drawn back for church but then pulled round to cover most of the walls for KidzClub and Toddler group making a brightly coloured hall for the activities.

You could have children's church before the main service, similar to the American style all-age Sunday school, with a worship session afterwards.

Lack of Experience or Training for Youth Work

The top qualification for youth work is to have a heart for the young people. Growing up in a harsh world with an increasing number of choices and issues is hard. Having someone around who cares is what most young people need.

If it is felt that some training or meeting people with experience in youth work will help, talk to someone from a local large church or your Local or Regional Team.

Go along to their youth evening or service and observe what they do and how the young people respond, or work alongside them in their young people's group on a Sunday for a period of time.

Ask the local youth worker to lead a day's training for you and people from other small churches who want to engage with youth.

Ask the large church which materials they successfully use in their youth small groups e.g. Youth Alpha, Youth Emmaus.

172

Things to Consider When Starting Children's or Youth Work

Read *Safe To Grow* (available from Baptist Union Publications).

Facilities

- Is there a room in the building not being used at present?
- Seating – appropriate sized chairs or floor (bean bags, carpet, mat).
- Entrance – should be manned.
- Games Equipment – child friendly and glass friendly, all in good condition.
- Toilets – should be accessible – never send more than one child at a time to the toilet and always escort young children.

Teachers

- Should be male and female.
- Must be Christian and preferably members of the church (although helpers could be non-Christian – some have come to faith through helping out then listening to what is being taught).
- Must be able to share their living faith with the children.
- There should always be more than one person with a class, preferably one of each sex.
- With children aged 5–10, the recommended minimum is one adult to every eight children. More adults are needed with younger children or if the group is going on an outing.
- Undergo a CRB enhanced disclosure before they start the work (as must all church leaders).
- Must have read *Safe To Grow* publication and put it into operation.
- Must meet together to plan and pray.
- Must have a good rapport with children and young people.
- Should receive training relevant to the age range and background of the children.
- Age needn't be a factor, but resilience is. Are your teachers/helpers likely to be seriously hurt if knocked over by an excited child? Older helpers can man 'quiet tables' for colouring and craft and

173

reading. The relationships formed can be invaluable to children who need attention and time to chat.

Children/Youth

- Under 6s can't usually cope with material designed for 6+, although 6–11s can work together.
- English as a second language needs noting as vocabulary will be limited. Use lots of visual aids.
- Special Needs require especially careful planning, make everything relevant.
- Disciplining needs planning, agreeing and all must adhere to it. It must be explained to the children (and to newcomers as they arrive).
- Each child/youth's name, address and emergency phone numbers must be kept on file by the Children's Team Leader and somewhere safely locked away on the church premises. Allergies and medical conditions should also be noted.

Materials

- Define which areas of Scripture you are going to teach.
- Define how you are going to teach to be relevant to each child.
- Connect with the children's or teenager's world, where they are, what they can identify with.
- Be culturally relevant – be careful with USA published materials.
- It should not resemble school – they go there all week, so try and avoid the words "Sunday School". Church classes should be built on relationships e.g. listening, discussing, being friends.
- Beware of programmes that just become entertainment.
- Use vocabulary in word and song that the children understand, not Christian jargon that is unfamiliar. Look at school assembly songs, they can be a good source and the children will already know them. Do the children like singing? Is it fun for them or just embarrassing?
- Must be straight forward and not too time consuming for the team to prepare.

Teaching

- Evangelistic and biblical but sensitive to the child's background.
- Knowledge based – teaching stories from the Bible, but not necessarily expecting children or young people to know facts and stories. Use memory verses with prizes.
- Time for Reflection – quiet reflection and discussion is an activity as much as games and crafts. Children need the space to think and ask questions about what they are learning and experiencing.
- Nurture – children with a church/Christian background who should know the basics can be encouraged to develop their spirituality and worship skills.
- Relationship Building – building trust between teachers, children and parents is vital. Children and young people need an adult they can trust and confide in, but be careful of promising confidentiality as they may tell you things that might need the intervention of the Police or Social Services. Praying with and for the children is good practice, so they can experience God's intervention first hand in their lives.

Be Aware . . .

- That children or teenagers will say anything (including "becoming a Christian") to please someone they like, without fully understanding what they are saying.
- Of the language you use as children will not understand concepts such as blessing, salvation etc. Remember we are living in a post-Christian society.
- That although we believe Christianity is the truth, we must show respect for other beliefs. Find out about other beliefs through a good book, not Christian gossip! Be clear when teaching that although we acknowledge that there are other religions, we believe that Christianity is the only way to God (The children and young people will have learnt about other faiths through the National Curriculum).
- That a badly run club will damage the Gospel's impact.

- That children have a short attention span and programmes should reflect this, no one section longer than 15 minutes.
- That materials, games etc need to be adapted for children with special needs. This also includes those who are more mature and very intelligent as well as those who are disabled and have learning/attention disabilities. Some children are used to having learning support at school so may need an adult "buddy" should a problem arise (A good resource is a book called *Special Children, Special Needs* by Simon Bass, Church House Publishing).
- Of talking down to children or teenagers giving simplistic answers.
- Of the amount of reading and writing required as this will put those with poorer skills at a disadvantage. They may then think that God does not love them because they can't understand or read.
- That people including children learn differently. Give a range of activities that cover the same story and get the children to choose how they want to learn. This prevents boredom setting in.
- Be cautious of using younger teenagers as teachers of under 5s. These are the most crucial developmental years of a child and therefore should have the most experienced of teachers. Teenagers should be used only in tandem with experienced teachers until they can get some basic training. Teenagers should never work unsupervised with children.
- Treat children and young people with respect and listen to them and they will respect and listen to you.
- If they ask a question and you don't know the answer say so, don't pretend or guess.
- Don't believe all they say, but never dismiss comments that could be about abuse or other problems.

Ideas to enhance work with Children and Young People

- We live in a visual age, so try to stimulate all senses.
- Ask about the children's favourite TV programme and adapt the answer to point to Jesus eg. DIY SOS which takes a disaster and

turns it into something new (as Jesus does with our lives) or Dr. Who, classic stories in which good triumphs over evil despite the odds.

- Pictures – OHP acetates, Powerpoint pictures of Cartoons/ Matchstick men/Flash cards/Story boards/Flannelgraph.
- Blackboard/flipchart or wipe board to write down answers.
- Physical ways to illustrate stories – Balloon modelling, Circus skills.
- Puppets and Muppets – get the children use the puppets to tell the stories, or teachers use the puppets to ask the children questions.
- Dressing up to be characters in the Bible stories using masks, wigs, hats, noses, glasses and random clothes.
- Objects – choose a relevant object to the story or discussions and ask for thoughts or reactions to it.
- Use colour as much as possible in classes.
- Interesting visitors for the children to "interview". Ask people in the church to take part. You could also invite Police Officers, Firemen etc.
- Videos are good for evening/midweek groups but tend to be too long for the Sunday mornings class.
- Maps to see where the story is taking place (Jerusalem, Israel etc) Get the children to appreciate distances such as where Paul travelled on his journeys.
- Drama/sketches are great for encouraging many skills such as performance, confidence, learning lines or working as part of a group. It is always good to perform a learned sketch to the whole church.
- Sign language to raise awareness of others disabilities and being part of the solution.
- The Bible!
- You – who you are and your faith make a huge difference!

CHAPTER SEVEN

WORKING TOGETHER

How good and pleasant it is when brothers live together in unity!
(Psalm 133v1)

Sharing Resources

Joshua said, "Remember the command that Moses the servant of the
LORD gave you: 'The LORD your God is giving you rest and has granted
you this land.' Your wives, your children and your livestock may stay in
the land that Moses gave you east of the Jordan, but all your fighting
men, fully armed, must cross over ahead of your brothers. You are to
help your brothers until the LORD gives them rest, as he has done for
you, and until they too have taken possession of the land that the LORD
your God is giving them. After that, you may go back and occupy your

own land, which Moses the servant of the LORD gave you east of the Jordan towards the sunrise."

Then they answered Joshua, "Whatever you have commanded us we will do, and wherever you send us we will go." (Joshua 1v12–16 NIV)

This command from God to "help your brothers" still stands today and speaks of mutual responsibility and support (The background story is in Deuteronomy 32). There are many ways in which churches could work together and sharing resources, such as sharing personnel, mission in the local area, joint services, amalgamating churches and freeing buildings or pooling money to pay for a youth worker. There are many innovative ideas being worked out in the UK between large / small churches, large / large churches and small / small churches, both within the Baptist family and ecumenically.

Two Baptist churches, each having 30 members, are on adjoining estates in Newport, Wales. Having a burden for older people and following a training day lead by Outlook Trust (a group specialising in evangelism among the elderly), they decided to put on a "Holiday at Home" week. They planned activities, meals and excursions for pensioners, with spiritual input. They were concerned about the practical workload of feeding large numbers for 5 days so they split the week between the two churches. Each church hosted 2 days and a trip was organised for the fifth day. The leadership teams met to pray and plan, sharing the booking of activities, applying for funding, arranging transport and finances. One church had catering equipment and tableware to lend the other, and the community links built by the second church's minister proved invaluable for obtaining funding and extra help. They learned not to compare resources but to focus on planning and working together.

The Bible gives us a few examples of working together for the gospel. Paul had told the churches in Macedonia and Achaia about the plight of the Christians in Rome and they wanted to help.

> Now, however, I am on my way to Jerusalem in the service of the saints there. For Macedonia and Achaia were pleased to make a contribution for the poor among the saints in Jerusalem. They were pleased to do it, and indeed they owe it to them. For if the Gentiles have shared in the Jews' spiritual blessings, they owe it to the Jews to share with them their material blessings. (Romans 15v25–27 NIV)

They had an attitude of "it's the least we can do" from the heart and gave with joy.

Apostles and prophets, letters and news travelled between churches in the early days, probably to encourage each other with stories not only of growth but also of endurance during tough times. "The churches in the province of Asia send you greetings. Aquila and Priscilla greet you warmly in the Lord, and so does the church that meets at their house. All the brothers here send you greetings" (1 Corinthians 16v19–20 NIV).

An area newsletter or meeting together to celebrate and swap news several times a year may seem small things but networking and regular communication is essential to counter feelings of isolation especially felt in the rural areas.

Be a Giving Church

In one small church, they had felt that an evening joint service on a regular basis with two larger local churches would be encouraging to all concerned. For the smaller church, it would fill the building to capacity, introduce them to other ways of worship and would be an opportunity to share the news of all three churches. It was organised and three well-attended services were held in one year. The next year, the larger churches decided not to continue with this and understandably the small church was disappointed and made a declaration in their next church meeting that when they reached 50 members, they would go out and help other small churches. However, God had other ideas and clearly said "Don't wait until then. I want you to start serving and blessing others now".

"Freely you have received, freely give" (Matthew 10v7–8 NIV).

How might we give and bless others? One way to give is to get involved with or even start a local network of churches, Baptist or ecumenical and take part in joint ventures. Another way is for a group of people to visit, with some regularity, another small church for a homegroup or a service to share testimonies about what God has done and is doing in their church and in the lives of individuals there. This can be enormously encouraging especially if it is the first time that the members of the group talk publicly about their faith, and they realise how God can use their stories to bless others (This activity could be the beginning of a partnership which grows over time covering many areas of church life).

The leadership of a small church should know the range of skills and abilities available, but is there a willingness to share those gifts with other churches who may be lacking in some areas, but possibly able to offer other gifts? Does your pastor preach at other small churches in the area? (It can be good to do a pulpit swap so the preaching is covered in both churches on the same day). Are there lay people who could preach or lead homegroups or courses at other local churches? Are there potential bookkeepers or even treasurers who could help out, or people with time and the ability to teach and care for the young or elderly, or are there people who could help with decorating and other "trade" work?

Each one should use whatever gift he has received to serve others, faithfully administering God's grace in its various forms. (1 Peter 4v10 NIV)

Share with God's people who are in need. (Romans 12v13 NIV)

Giving embraces the willing surrender of time, money, abilities, facilities (home or church) and convenience for the task of helping others in Jesus' name.

Be a Receiving Church

"In everything I did, I showed you that by this kind of hard work we must help the weak, remembering the words the Lord Jesus himself said: It is more blessed to give than to receive" (Acts 20v35 NIV). As Christians we have taken these words of Jesus to heart and many of us find receiving difficult, awkward or embarrassing, some even think of it as being sinful. However, for every giver, there must be a receiver and we must learn to accept gifts and compliments with grace.

As churches, we find it difficult to ask for help or receive it with grace when it is offered. Smaller churches often find the larger churches patronising in the way help is suggested, although receiving it may bring great blessing. It goes against our independent grain. However, church is family and working together and being interdependent is the way of the Kingdom. When another church offers help, it shows care and love and is often the start of bigger things when working together begins, however small the task at first. It is being open to new thoughts or ways of doing things and allowing another church to introduce these into our world. This is the beauty of clustering where churches communicate and work together, yet keep their identity in their local community. Remember the response to the gift is to give thanks to the giver and to the Lord, from whom all blessings flow.

Be a Sending Church

Be confident enough to be a sending church, releasing people to work elsewhere for God, as they were in Antioch. The church there prayed and fasted then obeyed God's call to send two of their best men on a journey to spread the gospel. What a challenge. It may be the call is for people to be sent abroad or to the small church across town. This act of obedience is especially hard if a small church only has two or three active and capable workers.

> As he looked up, Jesus saw the rich putting their gifts into the temple treasury. He also saw a poor widow put in two very small copper coins. "I tell you the truth," he said, "this poor widow has put in more than all the others. All these people gave their gifts out of their wealth; but she out of her poverty put in all she had to live on." (Luke 21v1–4 NIV)

However, God does operate the "echo" principle and blessings which are sent out, return multiplied.

> Give, and it will be given to you. A good measure, pressed down, shaken together and running over, will be poured into your lap. For with the measure you use, it will be measured to you." (Luke 6v38 NIV)

Clusters

These are groups of Baptist churches of various sizes within a geographical area who meet to pray, have fellowship and support each other in practical and spiritual ways. There are some very successful "clusters" of Baptist churches across the UK such as East Dartmoor Baptist Church.

East Dartmoor Baptist Church (EDBC) is an example of local congregations coming together for mutual support, to share ministry, and to encourage mission. It witnesses to the eastern edge of Dartmoor and some of the congregations have a long history. Old Church Minutes reveal small but faithful groups seeking to serve Jesus under difficult circumstances . . .

Read the full story in the Small Church Snapshot in Chapter 9.

The picture of apostles travelling frequently to encourage the churches sounds like a job description for Regional Team staff! They are people who have a bigger perspective of what God is doing in a geographical area and are able to make constructive suggestions and recommendations when visiting individual churches. It may be that within your area you have someone with the gift of encouragement who could visit a small group of churches, recognise their gifts and strengths and encourage them, as well as seeing areas for possible sharing. Someone maybe like Titus, a well known, praised and trusted figure in Asia Minor.

> I thank God, who put into the heart of Titus the same concern I have for you. For Titus not only welcomed our appeal, but he is coming to you with much enthusiasm and on his own initiative. And we are sending along with him the brother who is praised by all the churches for his service to the gospel. What is more, he was chosen by the churches to accompany us as we carry the offering, which we administer in order to honour the Lord himself and to show our eagerness to help. (2 Corinthians 8v16–19 NIV)

Partnerships

I was called from Duckpool Road Baptist Church into training for the ministry, and then into my first pastorate at Gaer Baptist Church. At the time Duckpool Road had over 100 members and was relatively affluent, whereas Gaer had just 17 members and was financially hard pressed. My link with the larger church where I had been ordained created an opportunity for partnership. In many ways this was a one way link, with Duckpool Road both lending and giving resources such as chairs, tables, OHP, technical help, spare hymn books etc to Gaer.

However, we did find a creative way of supporting ministry in the smaller church when I became a part-time pastoral worker for the larger church. This resourced Duckpool Road BC by easing the workload of the pastor, while also resourcing ministry in the small church by supplementing the limited stipend they were able to provide.

It is not easy for a small church to ask for help. I do not think the larger church would have been aware of Gaer's needs had there not been a personal link through me (and my gift for unashamed scrounging!) It may be that a relationship has to be formed at an individual or small group level before the needs are acknowledged and shared. It may be that a more solid foundation for the future is built this way rather than through a formally set up partnership.

Ruth Wood (Gaer Baptist Church)

In the Baptist Union Small Churches Report, there were frequent references to the issue of larger churches partnering to help smaller ones. Some of these were impassioned pleas, even delivered with a measure of resentment that churches that were well-resourced in terms of people and finance were ignoring the needs of their smaller sister churches.

By definition, this issue touches all of us, whether in a small church or a larger one. There is an obvious logic in resources being shared in order to shore up the work in a small church that may be at risk because its own resources are slim. However, large churches are invariably not looking enthusiastically for such partnerships, perhaps regarding them as a potential drain on their resources and a diversion from their particular calling.

Sometimes the pleas for help were qualified when fears were expressed that inviting a larger church for help would result in colonisation or even a takeover. Although this is an understandable fear, there may sometimes lurk behind it a desire to draft in people and perhaps money in order to perpetuate an unfruitful and maybe outdated model of church, without contemplating the possibility of substantial changes. It would be entirely unrealistic for a small church to think in these terms.

A healthy partnership needs to be based on mutual respect founded on mutual understanding. The "mutual understanding" is not to be taken for granted, as the dynamics of a small church will not necessarily be understood by people drafted in from a larger one. It also needs to be realised that a small church has qualities to offer a larger church, so there are relationship benefits for both parties.

In all this, Kingdom aims need to be paramount. It may be that the larger church will indeed lose some focus and the services of a number of its talented members, but if the end result is Kingdom expansion, then such sacrifices will have been worthwhile. Equally, the small church may have to accept new ways of doing things, along with the help that is offered, and this too needs to be taken on board for the sake of the Kingdom.

Despite these potential minefields, successful partnerships do exist between churches large and small, across the denominations and between churches or organisations in different countries. "Two are better than one, because they have a good return for their work: If one falls down, his friend can help him up" (Ecclesiastes 4v9 NIV).

Ecumenical Partnerships

Many small churches belong to their local Churches Together group to make an impact as Christians in the local area, and get involved with activities they could not do on their own. Working across the denominations also proclaims a powerful united message on the street. The effectiveness of the local ecumenical group often depends on the enthusiasm of the clergy and the relationships between them. In Kingston, Surrey, the local clergy from the central churches meet together every week for fellowship and to pray for their town, but most groups meet only three or four times a year. It is good to include both clergy and lay people at the meetings. Activities together vary considerably across the country and some ideas are listed in the Tools Section below.

It is important to be Kingdom-minded and work together with other Christian churches in the area to reach people with the good news. We're all on the same team! The theory is good but sometimes it is hard to maintain a Kingdom perspective when the large church down the road is growing and too busy with their programmes to even notice a small church. We must not let anger or envy get in the way of our mission being fulfilled. God treats each church differently and we may be in a strategic position or just have a heart for a specific people group, whereas the large church may be trying to cater for everybody.

Community Co-operation (Parish Planning)

Just suppose that yours is a small church in a smallish village. You have reasonable buildings, a coat of paint would not go amiss, but there is a kitchen, toilets, a few school rooms and of course the Chapel as everyone calls it. Also in the village, which does not have a school is the parish church (old and with no facilities at all), a flower club, a couple of people who (although you don't know it) used to play the piano, some recently retired men who you are told, "would not be seen dead inside a church" and a high proportion of elderly ladies, several of whom attend one of the two churches – Oh, and the Chapel grounds are a bit of a mess.

Well, that is where Community Co-operation, sometimes known as Parish Planning comes in. The idea is that your church would write to the parish church, the flower club, all the other clubs and societies in the village and post notices on the local boards saying:

This is who we are – a Baptist church.

This is what we do – worship on Sundays and try to serve the community.

This is where we meet – in the Baptist Chapel, (address).

This is what we have – some buildings, a kitchen, toilets, a piano and a photocopier.

This is what we need – someone to play for our services and to keep our grounds tidy.

And ask them to reply saying the same about themselves.

You then call a meeting for all those you have written to, whether they replied or not, plus everyone in the village. And what happens? Now imagine . . .

- That the Anglicans would love to run an old people's coffee morning which they would like to grow into a lunch club. They have the people but no facilities, could they please use yours; and of course your old people would be most welcome.
- That the flower club cannot find anywhere to meet. Could they use one of your rooms and in return, as they cannot afford much rent, they would do the church flowers for you once a month.
- That the gardening club would be happy to tidy up the church grounds so that the village can have a chance in the "village in bloom" competition.
- That two people say they wish your Chapel was open so that they could play the piano a bit; and in return over time offer to play once a month each at your services.
- That the secretaries of several organisations ask if they could use your photocopier to save having to drive into the next village every time.
- A couple of men say "don't ever expect us to come to your church but we could do a bit of decorating if that's any help". Similarly, the Anglicans ask whether the flower club would do the flowers for a forthcoming wedding and is there anyone who could take and circulate the parish annual meeting minutes?
- Two mums ask whether they could start an after school club using a Chapel room for homework.
- Much to your surprise a couple of teenage lads turn up asking whether their band could rehearse in your hall but cannot (or certainly do not) offer anything. They ask knowing that you will say "No" and are amazed ("gob-smacked" was their word), when having thought it through you say "Yes, and by-the-way we have an old pool table that no one uses and perhaps you might like to have a bit of fun with it!"

Now that may be a dream, but Acts 2v17 talks about visions and dreams as being associated with the Holy Spirit and, as T.E. Lawrence put it, ". . . the dreamers of the day are dangerous men for they may act out their dream and make it possible". Without dreams and visions the people perish, not just God's people but whole communities. Without acting out the dreams we cannot make them possible.

The concept of Community Co-operation is to build bridges to and within the community. It will work best in a village or other definable community with which people have a sense of identity. The offer that "this is who we are, what we can offer and what we want etc." must be open and without condition and other organisations encouraged to follow that lead. There will be disappointments and lack of responses in some places and from some people, including some of whom you had high hopes, but it is possible, just possible that a few weeks, months or years later you may be able to look back and see a village with a new sense of community and two churches more integrated into the life of the village and with more people and a range of activities "undreamed of" before.

Robert Kennedy once said "Some men see things as they are and say why?" I dream things that never were and say "Why not?" Is the Holy Spirit calling you to dream things that never were and ask "Why not?"

Twinning

The LORD said to me, "I have a greater task for you, my servant. Not only will you restore to greatness the people of Israel who have survived, but I will also make you a light to the nations – so that all the world may be saved." (Isaiah 49v6 TEV)

Twinning is a way of encouraging our churches to build a relationship with a church in another country so that each church fellowship can learn about the other country, the church situation there, church life and ministry and its joys and challenges. Working together might

189

include visits between churches, requests and answers to prayer and exchanging resources. This helps both churches to keep a global perspective on the Christian faith and explore new ways of being church. A set of guidelines for establishing an overseas partnership are in the Tools section below. There is a useful Baptist Union information leaflet called *Church Twinning* available. See the Snapshot below for how a small church started the twinning process.

Positive Partnership in Bristol by Neil Coulson, student minister of Stapleton Baptist Church

I write as the pastor of a small Baptist church to say how thankful we are at Stapleton Baptist Church for the better resourced, multi-staffed, larger membership Baptist Churches in neighbourhoods just a few miles away. On the important subject of how we work together as churches "big and small", whilst admittedly, there will be uninspiring and disappointing stories within the Baptist family, I write hoping that there are also plenty of positive stories of partnerships, like our own.

I am told that over recent years, the neighbouring larger churches have supported the life of our small church in many ways. But thinking of just the last two to three years, a respectable list of examples of support given by our sister churches is effortlessly collated: "Reserve" pianists, lay and ordained preachers, the loan of additional hymn books for our Christmas Nativity Service, Summer Club children's workers, a Youth minister's offer of Youth Alpha provision, their members supporting our monthly Saturday coffee morning. Additionally, one of the neighbouring church's ministers was partly responsible for a recent Mission Consultation here which led directly to the Church calling its first financially supported ministry since 1968.

It must be said that none of this support comes with any discernable sense of "throne" level condescension on their part. For the record, ministry here is also only possible because of the giving of other churches to Home Mission.

We thank God that our neighbouring churches are large, resourceful, multi-staffed churches. It strikes me that if they were not so, they would not be appropriately shaped for their own mission contexts and it would seem doubtful whether they could offer the same level of support to smaller churches like ours.

Cautionary Tale about a Church Partnership

This particular partnership was between a Home Mission funded project with a number of small churches and a large Baptist congregation approximately 10 miles away.

The link was made through the small churches' minister and one of the deacons from the large church. The large church subsequently found itself wanting to support a Home Mission project as part of its giving and approached the group of small churches to see if it was open to the idea.

The small churches were cautious as they did not want to be "taken over" or organised by the large church, but were otherwise in favour. The large church agreed not to exert undue influence over the small churches and set aside a budget for their support. Ways of exchanging practical support were also discussed so that it was not just a case of hand-outs being given to the small churches.

The partnership proved very effective in some areas. For example, the minister of the small church was able to organise mission events, with the large church agreeing to buy small items or materials needed or to underwrite some costs. A practical project to re-build some of the interior of one of the small churches was undertaken again with the support of the large church and this was particularly effective as, not only was there some financial support, but the large church supplied one person/labourer for every volunteer raised locally. It also acted as a bridge building exercise reaching non-church men who were happy to work on the project. The small church also benefited from the expertise of some of the large church volunteers. It was also possible for small church folk to attend some of the large church outreach events with guests. This meant that the small church did not need to organise the event themselves, they could spend their time with their guests instead, and the large church gained additional support for their events.

The areas of the partnership which did not work so well were the feedback of information on the situation at the small churches to the large church (this was wanted for prayer diaries so that the whole church could support in a non-financial way). The small churches did not manage to share their expertise with the large church. This was for a number of reasons – there were not very many people with the time available, and they were not aware of a need for their skills, and the large church seemed self-sufficient in this regard. Unfortunately there was also a fundamental difference in vision relating to mission between the small church and large church leaders. This meant that they had different priorities and wanted to pursue those.

What was learned?

1. It is important to set out the basis and working framework of the relationship early on, rather than leaving it to develop ad-hoc.
2. An expectation of a two-sided relationship and contribution to the partnership.
3. Good communication is essential.
4. Time needs to be allowed as a large church can take longer to make decisions with a larger structure and a small church can be too busy with its day-to-day activities to take time to plan activities which would include good strategic use of the large church help.
5. It is important to have one contact person on either side of the relationship. The small church person needs to be aware of the sensitivities of the small church and the needs of the large church. The large church representative needs to be aware of the way that decisions are made in a small church regarding informality and time-scales. This person needs to be reliable

and not too distracted by other demands from the large church as this can lead to small church information being lost amongst the mass of information circulating in a large church.

6. A list of the skills available in both the churches can prove useful.
7. Small churches need to realise that there can be differing opinions and visions regarding the partnership within the large church.

Whitemoor and New Basford Baptist Churches Nottinghamshire by Rev. John Huffadine, New Basford Baptist Church

Both of these small churches in the Nottingham area met regularly over some years as part of the local ecumenical group The Basford Forum.

The church in New Basford was being challenged to consider their future, with a building which was far too big for the small but committed fellowship of about twelve, and needing a considerable amount of money to bring it back to good order. They talked of closure and called the Regional Minister to pray and discuss the way forward with them.

One and a half miles up the road, the church at Whitemoor although also small, had a minister, who had recently retired from a full time job and now worked as pastor. The church was viable and trying to meet the needs of the community. Most of the twenty church members lived locally and walked to church.

As the relationship between the churches grew, they began to see the possibilities and positives of amalgamating. They met to pray, discuss and think about the future and shared services in both venues. Rev. Geoff Richards, a retired minister, proved to be a tower of strength to New Basford, taking on the role of pastor during this difficult period and helping with the decision making process. The leaders of both churches called in the Regional Minister in November 2003 who saw the great potential of this idea.

193

During the next 12 months, they had encouragement from the local Association, with a very good series of studies led by the local Mission Advisor. These were invaluable in helping to facilitate the courtship and marriage (as he put it) of the two fellowships, and helped them to put mission at the centre of the new church.

The two churches amalgamated in January 2005 with the new name of New Whitemoor Baptist Church. Not everyone from New Basford joined the new church. A few people did leave to join larger churches, but the majority stayed to be part of the "new thing" that God was doing. They have been so blessed in many ways. The two memberships quickly started functioning as one, determined to look to the future and not to the past. From the beginning the vision was to build an outward looking church, reaching out to those who had no church connections and presenting the gospel in a compelling way. They found that their different talents and gifts complimented each other, which enabled more mission to be done. With the impetus of the amalgamation they wanted to raise the church's profile and make the work and witness more effective. As a small "corner shop" church, they believe they have an important part to play within their local area of a large city.

They began a strategy called Meeting Our Neighbours, which involved an initial group of about 11 people knocking on doors to meet the local people and personally invite them to events held at the church. This new strategy was backed by the whole church in prayer and they have reaped rewards as people have come. They also have a puppet team who are regularly used in mission situations. They have a rolling three-year plan which focuses on mission in the local community.

The new church has plans to convert the existing building into a more up to date and purpose built place for their mission plans, which include a toddler group, a youth drop in, coffee shop and after school club. This will be mainly financed by the sale of the New Basford building.

This exciting story has seen a church which was considering closure but willing to leave their "home" for a future, and a church which was willing to take risks, to be transformed into a new re-energised people of God. There is now a buzz of excitement at this church, now at 34 members, as they fill the worship area with 50+ people on a Sunday morning, and look forward with hope to the future.

Long Whatton Baptist Church, Leicestershire by Rev. Mark Turner, Barrow on Soar Baptist Church

In 1997 it was decided that the small Baptist church in the village of Long Whatton should close, due to lack of numbers and an expensive building to maintain.

The East Midlands Baptist Association asked if any other Baptist church felt it right to replant the work. After much prayer and discussion, Barrow on Soar Baptist Church said "Yes", although they were 9 miles down the A6 on the other side of Loughborough. They redecorated and put new chairs into the small church, and an initial team of 25 members from Barrow recommenced the Sunday services there in April 1998. The team also instigated outreach into the village, meeting people door to door, running Alpha courses, fun days, quiz nights and barbecues. People came along and 2 were baptised.

During the next eight years, Long Whatton Baptist Church had 2 student pastors, the first for 5 years and the second for 3 years. They are presently without a pastor. The team from Barrow on Soar has changed over the years and there are now 12 people who work at Long Whatton regularly, alongside the elder.

The plan for the future is to employ a Community Worker to work one day a week (10 hours) to reach out to the young mums in the village through a mums and toddlers group.

The Baptists have built bridges with the other churches in the village, the Anglicans and Methodists, but sadly they are themselves in decline. There is determination though that the Christian witness will continue to reach the local population of 1300 people.

Long Whatton is a small and expensive village to live in so it hasn't been possible for the Barrow team to move there. It has been an experience for them of "doing mission from the outside". This is a story of perseverance where the work has evolved over a period of time. It has been said that it takes 10–15 years to plant and establish a church, and the pastor at Barrow would urge readers to be real about the time scale and not rush things.

Local support has been good and there is a new cluster forming at the time of writing called the Soar Valley Gospel Partnership. Its aim is to plant or replant churches in the area, (especially in the villages where churches have had to close) as well as support the existing churches.

Barrow on Soar Baptist Church currently has a membership of 146 people and their story of sharing resources to resurrect a small church is a shining example of the people of God working to establish the Kingdom of God.

Setting up a Local Ecumenical Partnership: Kirton in Lindsey, North Lincolnshire by Rev. Edith Dawson (now at Moss Side Church)

Kirton in Lindsey is a small historic town in North Lincolnshire, with around 3000 residents. When this story started there was an army barracks with some 800 soldiers and dependants, three churches (Methodist, Baptist and Anglican) and some local shops. The three churches did some work together but it was haphazard and echoed the division within the town. Jointly there were about seventy regular worshippers on a Sunday with an average of six children. (20 Methodists, 20 Baptists and 30 Anglicans)

The Minister and Deacons of the Baptist Church began to look at what they were doing. They were a small congregation of 20 people and had recently worked hard at making the chapel more attractive. How was it going to survive and did it have any future at all?

Sandy Harcus, the non-stipendiary Minister, thought that someone new had to come in to complement her and together they could make a difference in the community of Kirton in Lindsey. So began a conversation with the Regional Minister resulting in the decision to call Edith Dawson as three-quarter time minister. Funding from private sources was secured for three years with a possible extension to five but no more.

In the meantime a new Methodist Superintendent arrived and the Anglican Priest gave notice to leave at the end of the year. Edith arrived and spent her first year listening and attending all sorts of meetings in the community and the churches. The Anglicans called a new vicar and plans were already afoot for an outside nativity in the Market Place. The Churches worked together in a new way and the buzz was exciting.

Then a dream began to form that Edith shared with the others. The four church leaders went away for a day to talk and dream dreams facilitated by John Cole, Ecumenical Officer for All Lincolnshire. What emerged was the beginning of a new United Church as one by one the church leaderships embraced the dream and then envisioned the congregations.

Slowly over the next three years the churches moved from single services to united services, first once a month, then twice a month. Then the decision was made to declare intent to become a Local Ecumenical Partnership, moving towards a single congregation model, which they were already embracing.

This meant the children's work could be consolidated as they led the way having worshipped and learned together for four years. This led to youth work being developed, something none of the churches could do on their own. The Methodist Church made the brave decision to sell their building and the Baptists to convert their building into a Church/Community centre.

The constitution was drafted as were shared building agreements. As the end of year 4 approached for Edith, Home Mission was asked if they could enable her to stay longer to help the process along, which they did as, having visited, they caught the vision of God at work.

During this time there were difficulties around relationships in the town. The Town Hall needed some serious work to be done. Could it be used to bring the Town and the Churches together? The

Town Council did not get on with the trustees who did not get on with the Churches and here were three groups of people, with some commonality, yet with no cohesion. A Regeneration Partnership started and Edith represented the Churches, who were beginning to think strategically.

Relationships in the town changed as the Churches worked closer together, now as the United Mission Church of Kirton in Lindsey. The Army left to be replaced with the RAF and so the community continued to be vibrant and the church challenged by fresh insights into what it means to be a disciple in the 21st century.

During the next year, the Methodist Church reduced ministry and so allowed both Edith and the Anglican Rector to become authorised to serve in the town. However it seemed that the time had come to allow the new church to grow and call a new Minister who would have allegiance to the community of believers as first Edith gave notice and then the Anglican Rector.

The worshipping community increased, especially the family service, to around 120 and about 15 young people attending Junior Church. People remarked about the change in the Town Council and the Town Hall Trustees, who are now seeking funding for the work needed on the Town Hall. With vision and a lot of courage a small town has been changed by God's people working together.

The experimental church now has a life of its own as it seeks to serve and look to what the future brings. God does amazing things as we seek Him and remain faithful to the vision of a different future.

Twinning – "Into all the world" by Rev. David Priddy, Ashford Common Baptist Church

Ashford Common Baptist Church, a small church with about 20 members, has positively supported overseas mission projects since its formation. The support has generally been two-pronged. Firstly, we have provided a regular gift to a Port Missionary in Ireland who has visited us each year keeping us informed of the latest developments. Our financial gifts have been supplemented by providing small presents for the sailors to receive each Christmas.

Our second involvement has been to support an overseas mission project each Harvest and Christmas, to which our members have always given generously. We felt that God was directing us to be more focused in our giving, and to extend our thinking beyond a "give and forget" style to establish a link with another church. This would be as a partnership and enable members to relate more closely to what God was doing in another part of the world. As we developed a partnership, we would be able to provide tangible assistance to another church whilst we ourselves were enriched by the link.

It was agreed that we should draw up a likely profile of the partner church, including location, size, heart for God and community etc. and prayerfully seek God. Our prayer led us towards the Baptist World Alliance Congress in Birmingham, England in 2005 and so our pastor, David, went as a delegate and volunteer, whose first duty was welcoming other delegates to Congress. Having prayed before starting duty that God would lead him to a specific contact, he welcomed Pastor Timothy from Bangalore, India. Despite all the business of the day, there was a special sense of God being in this meeting. Contact details were exchanged before Timothy and David went their separate ways.

God has amazing ways of bringing people together. On the last morning David prayed that God would enable him to meet Timothy again should he be the link to this partnership. Being directed along a particular route, the two met and arrangements made for Timothy to visit our church before his return to India. Many from the church met Timothy, who described his conversion from Hinduism and the work of his church amongst the poor in Bangalore. We heard how they ran two schools, one for street children and one as a Christian-ethos school teaching a "normal" curriculum to those who would not otherwise be educated. We heard of the witness in their community and of the hardships they faced.

199

We heard of their prayer life and devotion to God. Above all, we heard from God that this was the church with whom we should build our partnership.

We found guidance notes on the "dos and don'ts" of overseas partnerships from a seminar helpful, which we adapted to a Baptist perspective (Copies of the notes are available from saxon5@bigfoot.com).

The Church members approved of the choice and sent David and one other leader (Martin) to verify the claims being made and take steps to establish the link. We decided that a week would be appropriate for this first encounter. In truth, neither relished the trip, but with much prayer backing, David and Martin enjoyed the time away and were kept free from any illness.

God blessed the week, which involved visits to the schools, ministry through three evening celebrations, a Home Group and Sunday Service. The blessing was mutual. We saw God move through the ministry times, the Indian people were hungry for God's Word and responded to it. Over 100 individual people asked for prayer at the conclusion of the meetings and some were won for Christ. A new Home Group was formed in the home of a Hindu lady who was freed from an evil spirit and the group is still flourishing. David and Martin were both influenced by the level of faith and dedication of the people.

One of the hallmarks of the church there is their prayer life. We know that when Pastor Timothy says that they are praying for us each day, it means that they do so in their daily prayer meeting from 5.30 to 7am each morning. Our church prayer life has been enhanced by the link with Bangalore. The majority of our Sunday evening meetings are now exclusively for prayer and primarily for the way ahead for our church. God has spoken to us in particular ways in these times.

The thought of forming a partnership was stimulated by reviewing our overseas mission giving, but the reader will have seen how our church's spiritual life has been enhanced. Turning lastly to the financial aspects, our annual freewill Christmas offering was allocated to establishing the project and covered the return air-fares, hotels and other expenses as well as enabling us to leave a gift in India.

At Easter we invited Church Members to give again. Our aim was to provide around £500 for all the books, resources and uniforms for the main school for the next academic year (July 2006–2007). In the event, the offering was sufficient to also pay for a move of the Street Children's School to larger premises (£250) and provided £250 of general support.

The Church has responded well in this first year of what is anticipated to be a long-term partnership and there is an over-riding sense of being part of the church worldwide.

TOOLS FOR WORKING TOGETHER

Questions

This list of questions is designed to be considered by the Church Leadership.

- Is your church in a cluster or partnership? If yes, does it have mutual benefits?
- How could it be enhanced and expanded?
- Is there good communication between parties and if not, how could they be improved?
- If the local partnership is successful, could the concept be adopted to partnership overseas?
- If an overseas partnership is successful, could the concept be adopted to partnership locally?
- If not in a cluster or partnership, have you ever considered the idea? Do contact your Regional Minister to discuss possibilities.
- What areas of your church work could you offer to help other churches?
- How does your church feel about asking for help?
- What areas of your church work would be better with others to share with or help you?
- What could be done better or more effective in your locality if you worked with another local church?
- Has the Parish Planning article inspired you to impact your town or village?
- Is your church part of a Churches Together group?
- Do the local ministers/leaders meet together, either Baptist or ecumenically?
- Does the idea of interdependence rather than independence sound good?

Could your church surrender its independence and opt into connecting fellowships together locally? Keep its character and history but share the future. What terms would you want to apply and would it be reasonable for other churches to apply the same terms?

For Discussion in Small Groups

1. Compare Joshua 1v14b–15 with Philippians 2v1–4. How can we live this out as individual believers? As local churches?
2. Read Paul's description of an unselfish church in 2 Corinthians 8v1–5. What can we learn from the Macedonians about supporting other Christians?
3. Can you name 3 Baptist Churches nearest yours? How are they getting on, what is their vision and what challenges are they facing? If you don't know, what could you and your church do about it?
4. What are our church's priorities in developing and using our resources (funds, equipment and facilities, people's time and abilities)? Do our priorities fit with the command in Joshua 1v15?
5. Can we / should we change what we are doing in order to help our brothers? Read Number 32v16–18. Can we come up with a good compromise for our church?

Ideas for working together ecumenically in the local area

- Holiday Clubs.
- Giving a gospel or Jesus Video to every household in the village/town.
- March and/or service of witness on Palm Sunday, Good Friday or Easter Sunday.
- Christmas Carol singing at a local supermarket, or round a Christmas tree in town.
- New Year celebration.
- Ecumenical coffee shop or drop-in centre.
- 24-hour prayer week for the town.

- Paying for Christian books to be placed into the local library.
- Host a mission e.g. On the Move, J.John's Just 10 missions (based on the 10 commandments).

For more information about Churches Together contact Churches Together in England www.churches-together.org.uk.

Some Guidelines for Twinning with a Church Overseas

Pray – Twinning can be a fun idea but it must be God's plan. Let Him show you which country or person to link with.

Define the Relationship – are you looking for a mutual link or a "charity" link?

Should we be looking to partner inside our denomination/grouping, any church or an organisation?

Once you have chosen a partner church, then ask:
Is the overseas church partnered with anyone already? If so, how does this affect the relationship?

Are they looking for a mutual relationship with you or just material help?

What are the expectations on both sides? Draw up short and long term goals.

What are the benefits to both sides? These could be:

- Prayer Partnership.
- Money.
- Skills.
- Teaching a world perspective – being part of a global church.
- Cross cultural understanding.
- Challenge to materialism.
- Joy in giving.

How are we going to run the project – visits, prayer letters on the internet, regular money etc.

Who is going to visit? It is wise to send a couple of leaders to check out the overseas situation before a formal partnership is made. Experiencing their worship, study and work at first hand is essential.

How often will the visits be? Annually?

Are you going to set up a new local project together, or just support what they are doing already?

How can the church members of both sides be involved?

Be Aware . . .

- A partnership is long term.
- Of assuming our culture or the way we do things is correct. Don't be arrogant but humble and always ready to learn. Exercise Kingdom culture.
- The way money is handled is different in different countries, budgeting may be a new concept and accepting bribes normal! Always be people of integrity and not compromising scriptural values. Always give money to the church, not individuals.
- About taking God's place of being their provider. Be wise in your generosity.
- Social values and family life can be very different.

CHAPTER EIGHT

PLACES TO WORSHIP AND WITNESS

In the Bible, God was worshipped: On a mountain

Then Moses led the people out of the camp to meet with God, and they stood at the foot of the mountain. Mount Sinai was covered with smoke, because the LORD descended on it in fire. The smoke billowed up from it like smoke from a furnace, the whole mountain trembled violently, and the sound of the trumpet grew louder and louder. Then Moses spoke and the voice of God answered him. (Exodus 19v17–19 NIV)

In the Tent of Meeting

Now Moses used to take a tent and pitch it outside the camp some distance away, calling it the "tent of meeting". Anyone enquiring of the LORD would go to the tent of meeting outside the camp. And whenever Moses went out to the tent, all the people rose and stood at the entrances to their tents, watching Moses until he entered the tent. As Moses went into the tent, the pillar of cloud would come down and stay at the entrance, while the LORD spoke with Moses. Whenever the people saw the pillar of cloud standing at the entrance to the tent, they all stood and worshipped, each at the entrance to his tent. The LORD would speak to Moses face to face, as a man speaks with his friend. (Exodus 33v7–11 NIV)

In the Tabernacle

Then Moses set up the courtyard around the tabernacle and altar and put up the curtain at the entrance to the courtyard. And so Moses finished the work. Then the cloud covered the Tent of Meeting, and the glory of the LORD filled the tabernacle. (Exodus 40v33–34 NIV)

In the Temple

When Solomon had finished building the temple of the LORD and the royal palace, and had achieved all he had desired to do, the LORD appeared to him a second time, as he had appeared to him at Gibeon. The LORD said to him: "I have heard the prayer and plea you have made before me; I have consecrated this temple, which you have built, by putting my Name there for ever. My eyes and my heart will always be there. (1 Kings 9v1–3 NIV)

In Synagogues

As his custom was, Paul went into the synagogue, and on three Sabbath days he reasoned with them from the Scriptures, explaining and proving that the Christ had to suffer and rise from the dead. "This Jesus I am proclaiming to you is the Christ," he said. (Acts 17v2–3 NIV)

In Homes

Paul, a prisoner of Christ Jesus, and Timothy our brother, To Philemon our dear friend and fellow-worker, to Apphia our sister, to Archippus our fellow-soldier and to the church that meets in your home. (Philemon v1–2 NIV)

In the Street

The apostles performed many miraculous signs and wonders among the people. And all the believers used to meet together in Solomon's Colonnade. (Acts 5v12 NIV)

In the Church (people)

Yet a time is coming and has now come when the true worshippers will worship the Father in spirit and truth, for they are the kind of worshippers the Father seeks. God is spirit, and his worshippers must worship in spirit and in truth." (John 4v23–24 NIV)

In Heaven

At once I was in the Spirit, and there before me was a throne in heaven with someone sitting on it. And the one who sat there had the appearance of jasper and carnelian. A rainbow, resembling an emerald, encircled the throne. Surrounding the throne were twenty-four other thrones, and seated on them were twenty-four elders.

Each of the four living creatures had six wings and was covered with eyes all around, even under his wings. Day and night they never stop saying: "Holy, holy, holy is the Lord God Almighty, who was, and is, and is to come." Whenever the living creatures give glory, honour and thanks to him who sits on the throne and who lives for ever and ever, the twenty-four elders fall down before him who sits on the throne, and worship him who lives for ever and ever. They lay their crowns before the throne and say: "You are worthy, our Lord and God, to receive glory and honour and power, for you created all things, and by your will they were created and have their being." (Revelation 4v2–4a, 8–11 NIV)

In the 21st century

God is not constrained by location and, as He is omnipresent, we can worship Him anywhere. It is however, helpful to have a building in which to worship together and for people in the community to know where they can find God's people. Buildings can have an atmosphere of worship and a hushed awe of God about them and the prayers of the saints down the ages can be felt emanating from the walls in some older churches. From grand cathedrals to the local small church, the building is a public place where God meets people and an excellent location for activities in which to serve the community and make Jesus known.

Lunches, Parent and Toddler groups, coffee mornings, Alpha Courses, teaching English and IT skills, providing clothes washing facilities and toy libraries are just a few of the ways in which God's people are using their buildings.

The general understanding in society is that a church is a building. For congregations, especially smaller ones that meet in other locations, such as schools, youth or community centres etc, potential visitors don't think it's a "proper" church. While the hiring of such locations can be helpful, especially with church plants, it can hinder midweek and evening activities. It also hinders a sense of "sacred space" in a room, which has many uses during the week. Conversely the benefit of not owning a building is that the money otherwise tied up in or spent on the fabric can be spent on training and mission.

Buildings can be a great blessing but can be a real drain on limited resources. In the Tools section is a survey of church facilities and it is often the case that a small amount of money spent such as a coat of paint can make a big difference to appearance. There are also suggestions of help with funding for buildings in Chapter 9. Radical thinking like amalgamation with another small church can change a gloomy situation such as an expensive or crumbling building, into a new beginning.

The Church is not a Building by Rev. Catriona Gorton, Hugglescote Baptist Church

The church is not a building,
The church is not a steeple,
The church is not a resting place –
The church is PEOPLE![1]

I learned this song 20 years ago as a Sunday School teacher in a small Baptist church in Derby. I loved the theology then, and I love it now, not least because as the minister of a small Baptist church who had to close a much-loved building, it is a theology we have to live.

I arrived at Hugglescote Baptist Church in January 2004. Six months later a routine insurance inspection of our building identified several areas that required immediate attention. After various inspections, that cost about £3000, we were forced to leave the building immediately. Problems with the fabric included:

- Dangerous gas equipment and many aspects of installation illegal (the presence of asbestos made servicing the boiler very difficult).
- Obsolete wiring, not compliant with current standards (about £1000 was spent on essential work before it became clear that the building would have to close) and a full rewire was needed.
- Wet rot, dry rot, beetle infestation, woodworm, penetrating and rising damp.
- Problems with guttering, pointing and decayed brickwork.

---

[1] Richard K Avery and Donald S March, *I am the Church*, Hope Publishing Company, 1972.

The total estimated cost of refurbishment, including provision of minimal disabled access which the building did not have, was around £200,000. The site value, as it stood, was £200,000 (though the estimate for a cleared site with outline planning for housing is potentially twice that). Superficially the inside of the "sanctuary" looked quite good – it was clean and in fairly good decorative order, masking the decay that was evident on closer inspection such as mould on the vestry walls . . .

Our Anglican friends generously lent us their building for our Christmas services. After the holiday period we moved into the hall of the local primary school, where we have been ever since. Our church meetings are held at the local Methodist Church hall, our children's games club meets in the primary school; most other activities have moved into members' homes.

Early in 2005 after surveys, quotations for remedial work and a site valuation we realised that the building would have to close permanently. This decision was not taken lightly. Many had known no other place of worship: here they had been baptised, married, brought their babies for blessing and said farewell to parents or partners. Others had mixed feelings – sadness at the end of an era but relief that the burden of caring for the fabric had ended. In June 2005, our Regional Minister preached at a service of thanksgiving for the building, using the Emmaus Road story to help us understand how sadness could turn to joy with Jesus as our travelling companion.

At the time the building closed, we had two congregations each of around 20, with little overlap. The morning congregation attracted the younger people and was slightly more contemporary in style than the evening, which was very traditional.

The age profile is definitely older rather than younger, with a range from early 40s to mid 90s and most aged over 70 (around twice as many women as men). Of the women who come alone, about half are widowed and half have partners who do not attend church. Many questions arose following the closure of our building and we continue to work at and review the way forward in a whole range of areas.

Our worship life changed dramatically when we combined our morning and evening congregations into one, now meeting in the afternoon. We set out enough chairs for our needs, which feels very different from a church built for 600. Our service style has evolved from traditional to structured informal and I am blessed with a congregation who will try most things.

Closing the building affected our mission work. The church had a bi-monthly lunch club and we had planned to start a weekly "drop-in" cafe at Easter 2005. Neither was now possible, and this raised many questions about God's will for us. With some creativity, a small team came up with a new idea, and in autumn 2005 Hugglescote PLUS+, was launched in association with Leicestershire Social Services. Once a month, we bus 50 senior citizens for a restaurant meal and sometimes a speaker. It is great fun, and gives us opportunities to build relationships with coach drivers and restaurant staff as well as our guests.

In December 2005 we held a community event, linking up with Real Christmas, a radio broadcast Carol Service. We hired the Community Centre, laid on a free tea for our PLUS+ friends and craft activities for children, with the broadcast service and free festive refreshments to follow. About 120 people came – four times our usual congregation!

To follow this, in June 2006 we held a Pentecost Party Weekend. On the Saturday we arranged a free fun day for the local community. We invited local craftspeople, a dancing school and a youth rock band to put on displays. Around 20 of us, with a few folk borrowed from other local churches, staffed the tea tent, face painting, bouncy castle and games. Over 200 people came along for a fantastic afternoon. On the Sunday we had an open air Pentecost service attended by 50 people including about 12 people with no known church connection.

When we moved out of our building, we used the story of Moses and the Israelites leaving Egypt to help us see how God is present during times of uncertainty and disorientation. We noticed how they did not know at the start how long the journey would take, and certainly did not take the shortest route across the wilderness. Sadly we have lost one or two people since leaving our building but an equal number have joined us on the way.

Home Mission funding is vital! Our income would not support full time ministry and the congregation feel they need a full time minister if they are to do anything more than simply survive. It became clear that the building issues were gobbling up all our reserves of cash, so we recently applied for HM funding to sustain full time ministry and enable us to do mission work. We feel we are caught between a rock and a hard place: we cannot grow without doing mission, we can't do mission without both a minister and money, but we cannot afford both unless Home Mission can help us. I feel that the giving by my congregation is good given our size and socio-economic mix, and do not see that asking people to increase their giving as appropriate.

The future for our church is far from clear. Sometimes I feel like a juggler, trying to keep many balls in the air, as we work at selling our building, developing our mission in this community, playing an active role in Churches Together and discussing closer working with another small Baptist church. Yet, overall I am inspired and encouraged by what we have, with God's help, achieved together.

Sometimes I get cross and frustrated, bowed down by the criticisms and grumbles of the few. Sometimes the enormity of the task and vulnerability of my own post as minister frighten me. Mostly, I am proud of the courage of my congregation and marvel at the crazy, wonderful God who trusts someone like me to serve them. My congregation know that my favourite Bible verse is James 2v26 – "faith without deeds is dead" – and my choice of Bible readings for my ordination was the Great Commission (Matthew 28) and the Parable of the Sheep and Goats (Matthew 25). Put these with the images of the church as a body (Romans 12 and 1 Corinthians 12) and you begin to understand my thinking!

Church buildings can be useful but God is not constrained by them. When our building had to close, we left our comfort zones

213

to discover that God was already active "out there" – and we joined in. Jesus said "Go . . ." – we're going and it's exciting!

Village Film Night at Feniton by Rev. Graham Parkinson, South West Baptist Association

What do you do when a village chapel is no longer viable as a place for Sunday worship? The easy answer is to "close and dispose" and this happens, and is often the appropriate course of action.

One such Chapel was situated in the little village of Feniton just west of Exeter, Devon. The Membership had dropped to two and they were elderly, there was no energy left and it reached the critical closure figure. The trustees, the South West Baptist Association Corporation however, had the vision to ask if the site had actually finished its potential for outreach. After prayer walking around the community's new housing projects it was obvious that it was an expanding village, being a satellite for two major urban conurbations. It was decided to spend a modest amount on refurbishment, and set a period of time to "test the water".

The chapel was initially reopened to show films once a month, based on a similar project that had been successful in another local church. We had a spot at the assembly of the local school hoping to attract children from the community and the outlying areas who attended the school. Instant success! On the first day armed with our CCL copyright license and data projector we planned an early film for the young ones then a later film for young teens, all the fruit they could eat, and chips in the interval from the local pizza place. We'd hoped for 20, and the children started to arrive, they came and came, and at 45 it was obvious that there were too many for the building and we had to promise the last few another showing the following week.

We found out that three teachers at the school were Christians who had been praying for something just like this. There are now around 100 children on the books and a host of grateful mums, dads and grandparents. The kids have fun too! One parent said that to take the whole brood to the cinema in town would cost something like £30. Other events are in the planning stage, perhaps Holiday Clubs and a Bible club. We are humbled yet again by the power of prayer and encouraged that if God is in the plan anything is possible.

God's Blueprint for our Church by Aline Fynn, Hammersmith Christian Fellowship, London

After 40 years, our Pastor retired so the church family came together to agree a Mission Statement and seek God's way forward. At the time (1995), we had about 18 members and an average attendance of 25 people.

Our building was falling down and there were too few workers to manage it. Repairs were too costly and anyway, without substantial redevelopment and spending millions of pounds, the building would never be user-friendly: i.e. the outside toilets were to the rear; the main hall was up two flights of concrete stairs, and the cumbersome corridors and very high ceilings meant most of our heating was lost.

The vision some of us began to share was to have a building open every day for Jesus, a building full of worshipping people from many nations, of all ages and abilities, serving God, each other, and the community in whatever way would best meet their needs. We knew we had to do something radical. So we sought the Lord. Should we move? We looked for other properties in the area. Should we sell part of the building? Which bit? The sanctuary area lent itself best for housing and would probably be easier to sell, and yet it seemed this was the part God wanted for His particular use.

Some of our fellowship felt God was leading them on a different journey and it was difficult for us to let them go to other churches. Some of them felt that God had completed a very successful work at our church and that we should sell up completely and move on individually to work for God in other churches. This left us with

215

6 church members and a congregation of 12, some of whom were people who worshipped with us either on a Sunday or during the week who would find it difficult to settle anywhere else.

In September 2000 the Trustees of the church made this statement: "We feel that your church is no longer viable and would like to talk to you and the other leaders of the church about its future".

I could understand where the comment was coming from. However it seemed to be entirely from a human point of view and some of us felt strongly that God had other ideas for our fellowship. As the elder I presented a case to the trustees to demonstrate why we as a small church should be allowed to go ahead with elaborate plans to redevelop and remould our building for Christ.

For the church family who remained, man's logic was understandable, but God's vision seemed even more real. The building is situated within a community which has a varied Christian witness, and there is definitely a place for our multicultural family who enjoy a unique form of traditional and contemporary music and open worship within the community. We believed God still had a work for us to do.

God provided a building contractor who wanted to buy the back of our building and was willing to develop the sanctuary area to our specification with a mezzanine floor, halls, disabled facilities etc. as part payment. The Council would not give us permission to change the appearance of the windows nor were we able to remove or replace the railings. Working within those restraints was not easy, especially when everything that was done had to comply with multiple regulations. Plans had to be changed several times and rooms moved to facilitate lift motors and systems. God provided the right contractors to work with us. They patiently waited whilst the viability of our project was addressed, and showed sensitivity and care in all the works they undertook. After everything was in place, including all kitchen appliances, decoration, carpets etc. the contractors gave the church a monetary balance of approx £50,000. The church used this to pay off the loan on the manse and used the rest of the money towards a new Pastor.

We had proved that our God is faithful and that in ALL THINGS He works for good. We praise God that the trustees allowed us to go ahead with the project.

Each time we, as a church family, were unsure what to do next, God showed the way. Each time we needed encouragement, God sent along someone, who usually knew nothing of our situation, to build us up and give us that word in season. Our experience certainly taught us to depend on God in all things; we brought prayer to the top of our agenda and I believe we can all say we grew in God. We had to learn to trust God when the way looked impossible. Key words which describe the family who worship at HCF now are UNITED in LOVE.

It has been said that we were like the seed that had to fall into the ground and die in order that God could bring forth new life. We have sometimes felt like the stump described in Isaiah. We always knew God had plans and purposes for us. We claimed Jeremiah 29v11 for ourselves: " 'For I know the plans I have for you,' declares the Lord, 'plans to prosper you and not to harm you, plans to give you hope and a future'". The vision we received from Him in 1995 has grown stronger rather than fainter as we have moved nearer our goal.

Our building has totally changed on the inside, but the people within the building have been changed too, from the inside out by God. Our attitudes, outlook, perceptions, expectations; we know this is a continuing work because God has a real job for us to do. Yes, we are far from perfect but everyone is involved to a greater or lesser degree and is prepared to use their gifts for God.

We recognise that now we have a redeveloped and practical building, the real work has begun. We have no more excuses for not reaching out and there are the faithful few here who are raring to go! And we are growing. We are blessed with friends who pray for us and support us by their presence from time to time. We have a weekly Prayer meeting and Bible Study, a Lunchtime Fellowship, and a thriving Carer and Toddler group. We hope to begin a youth group soon, initially to retain the youth we have and then to encourage them to bring friends. But remember we still only have 16 members!

These are exciting and challenging times for us so we say to God "we are here and available – use both us and this wonderful building which you have given to us"

BUILDING TOOLS

Questions about Church Buildings

This list is a basic set of questions about church buildings. The remainder of the Tools assume that you have a building of some sort.

- Does your church own a building for worship?
- Does your church own a hall and other facilities?
- If your church does not own a building, consider the positives and negatives of owning one.
- Does your church own a manse/vicarage?
- Is your manse/vicarage occupied?
- If it is empty, would you consider renting it?

Suggestions

This list of suggestions is designed to be considered by the Church Leadership.

How can a Small Church best use their building?
Before looking at any of the points below, it maybe wise to find out whether your church building is listed. It will affect what you can do, what you need to get permission for and how much VAT you may have to pay.

On more substantial works and the hiring out of premises, it is likely that you will need to get the consent of the Holding Trustees (being those people or that body that legally and technically owns the building and land). Before hiring out you should certainly take legal advice, leases can be tricky things.

Funding for building projects may be available (see chapter 9). Good or bad messages are conveyed by the building, both inside and outside and sometimes a small amount of money, even just repainting the external doors, will rectify wrong impressions.

Bear in mind that without reasonable, hygienic (and preferably warm) kitchen and toilets, the buildings are of little use and are very likely to put off any visitors.

- Get an architect or a building specialist not familiar with your buildings or fellowship or premises, to look at your buildings and give you real options and their cost. Be imaginative when consulting them, such as using roof space, mezzanine floors etc.
- Replace pews with chairs and use the space differently. If the pews are on raised pew platforms some investigation is needed before starting work (what is under the platforms, how is the building heated etc.).
- Merge with other church/churches and sell buildings using the money for resources, refurbishment.
- Mothball or even demolish totally unwanted and perhaps derelict buildings.
- Sell half the building to developers.
- Sell the building and rent one locally for services only e.g. school, youth centre, pub or theatre. Bear in mind that renting space increases the preparation time before a service or activity – chairs, tables, other equipment have to be brought out of storage or from elsewhere and set out, then put way afterwards. You need able-bodied people to do this, so it could be a problem for an ageing congregation. Arrangements can be made with caretakers for a fee.

A Facilities Survey

Get a not-yet Christian friend to critically go round your church building with, or perhaps without, you noting all the points that need change or updating, and answering the questions below. On their first visit people tend to notice the entrance area, toilets, the coffee and the kitchen if they get that far.

How many days a week is the building used?
How many hours a week is your building used?

What do you use the building for?
What would be a visitor's first impressions?

Notice boards.
Are the church building and notice board visible from the street? Watch out for "unwelcoming" notices such as the one which says "Don't enter if there is a prayer or Scripture reading going on" – these are common in older chapel entrances.

Front entrance.
State of outside appearance – clear up litter around the entrance. Pots of flowers are cheap and attractive and make the church look cared for.

It is inevitable that the main church doors will be shut most of the time, which tends to make churches look unwelcoming, so anything that overcomes this impression is beneficial. If it is possible to install glass doors and have some lights on inside so that the building at least looks lived in is one way of achieving this.

What facilities does the building have?

Kitchen.
Hall.
Meeting Rooms – how many?
Toilets.
Provision for the disabled, old people and mums with buggies and young children.

What state of repair/disrepair is the building in?

What is the cost of making repairs?
How much is spent per annum at present?
What percentage of the church income is that?
How much would be needed to put the buildings into good repair?

How often are the gutters and rainwater pipes checked and cleared?

When was the building last decorated inside/outside?

When did you last redecorate your home inside/outside and what might that say?

Prioritise the repair work and re-cost it.

Where can we find appropriate workmen to do the repairs?

What repairs could we do ourselves?

Are there men in the area who, while not church attenders, would be willing to help? (This is not a sexist comment, but men will often be willing to work in a church but not worship there). Approaching them in this way can be a useful bridge to them and their circle of friends.

How is the building heated and how much does it cost per year?

What is the financial status of the church?

Are the buildings adequately insured?

What type and how much space is there outside the building? Grass, hard surface, garden, walls or fencing, gates. How well are they maintained and what does that say about the church?

Where is the building located? City, village centre, residential, rural, other.

Have the people moved away from the church as the area has changed and developed? Should the church go to them rather than expect the people to come to church?

Remember, Jesus said "Go".

What are the needs of the community? Carry out a survey door to door in the local streets or talk to the Local Council and Social Services.

How do you put the community needs and your building together?

Suggestions for Community Uses of the Building

Here are a few ideas that might be worth considering for the increased use and mission of your church buildings. Several will need consents before they can be started e.g. Hygiene requirements for activities involving food preparation and serving. This list is by no means exhaustive, although some activities may be exhausting!

- Coffee morning.
- Parents and Toddlers group.
- Adult and Children's craft classes.
- Lunch club and entertainment for older/lonely people.
- Flower festivals.
- Tea dances.
- Meeting place for self-help groups e.g. Alcoholics Anonymous.
- Internet café.
- Polling station.
- Post Office.
- Farmers market.
- Art exhibitions.
- Centre for blood donation.
- Social Services weekly clinics.
- Contact centre for separated families.
- Local meetings e.g. neighbourhood and police meetings, Neighbourhood Watch.
- After school or homework clubs.
- Invite local schools to join you for Harvest, Christmas and Easter services.
- Men's breakfasts.
- Parenting classes.
- Youth and/or unemployed drop-in.

CHAPTER NINE

HELP! AND RESOURCES

Consultancy

The Baptist Union run a Consultancy for Mission programme, which enables a church to have a health check. The Methodist Church runs a similar scheme. The consultants can be invited to come to the church at any time, though often they are invited in a time of interregnum when the church needs to seek God for the way forward. The church contacts the Regional Team who recommend two appropriate and trained consultants to visit. A small church applying for a consultation should be sent at least one consultant with experience in a small church.

The consultants have a questionnaire, which the church completes, with questions about the internal running of the church, the use of the buildings, the financial position and the community the church is reaching.

People from outside the situation can often help a church see the wood from the trees by asking apparently simple/innocent questions that can open up fresh insights and ideas. Sometimes the effect can be of liberation from the past and past expectations. This may be a form of permission-giving to discontinue outmoded patterns of work and to experiment creatively. The consultation usually consists of:

- A meeting between the consultants and the church leaders.
- A day led by the consultants for the whole church.
- A meeting when the findings report is given to the church leaders, with the consultants recommendations for the future.
- The consultants will keep in touch as appropriate or as the church requests. A visit in a year's time is usual.
- The church can use the report in writing a church profile if they are applying for a new minister, or showing the extent of mission when applying for denominational funding.

Contact your Regional Team for more details.

Charities, Trustees and Trusteeships

Virtually all churches are charities, although up to now most of them have been classed as "excepted" which meant that they did not have to register with the Charity Commission. As from 1st April 2008 those with an income of over £100,000 will have to register and those with a smaller income will be required to register in due course.

Charities are "managed" by trustees. Thus virtually all churches should have trustees; they are usually known as Charity (or Managing Trustees) and are made up of the minister and deacons, elders or other leaders. If the church owns land and buildings, they are required legally to have a second set of Trustees known as Custodian or Holding Trustees.

Charity Commission Guidelines

The Charity Commission published a booklet in 2005 entitled *CC3 – The Essential Trustee: What you need to know*. This replaced their guidance leaflet CC3 Responsibilities of Charity Trustees (March 2002).

Charity/Managing Trustees

These consist of the minister, whether ordained or lay, and deacons and/or others who are responsible for the day-to-day management of the charity (the church). The words now used by the Commission are Charity Trustees.

Trustees and their responsibilities (as set out by the Commission)

Charity Trustees are the people who serve on the governing body of a charity. They may be known as Trustees, Directors, Board Members, Governors or Committee Members (and in a church context Deacons, Elders, Leaders etc.). The principles and main duties are the same in all cases.

Trustees have and must accept ultimate responsibility for directing the affairs of a charity, and ensuring that it is solvent, well-run, and delivering the charitable outcomes for which it has been set up.

Compliance – Trustees must:

- ensure that the charity complies with charity law, and with the requirements of the Charity Commission as regulator; in particular ensure that the charity prepares reports on what it has achieved and annual returns and accounts as required by law.
- ensure that the charity does not breach any of the requirements or rules set out in its governing document and that it remains true to the charitable purpose and objects set out there.

- comply with the requirements of other legislation and other regulators (if any) which govern the activities of the charity.
- act with integrity, and avoid any personal conflicts of interest or misuse of charity funds or assets.

Duty of prudence – Trustees must:

- ensure that the charity is and will remain solvent.
- use charitable funds and assets reasonably, and only in furtherance of the charity's objects.
- avoid undertaking activities that might place the charity's endowment, funds, assets or reputation at undue risk.
- take special care when investing the funds of the charity, or borrowing funds for the charity to use.

Duty of care – Trustees must:

- use reasonable care and skill in their work as Trustees, using their personal skills and experience as needed to ensure that the charity is well-run and efficient.
- consider getting external professional advice on all matters where there may be material risk to the charity, or where the Trustees may be in breach of their duties.
- *Note:* use of the word "must" means it is a specific legal or regulatory requirement affecting Trustees or a charity.

Custodian or Holding Trustees

These are the terms used to describe the trustees or trustee body that hold the church's property [land and buildings]. The above mentioned Charity Commission leaflet gives the following definitions:

A Custodian Trustee is a corporation appointed to have the custody, as distinct from the management, of trust property. Where a Custodian Trustee is appointed to hold property of a charity, the administration of the charity is left in the hands of the Charity Trustees. A Custodian Trustee is not a Charity Trustee.

Holding Trustees are individuals appointed to hold the property of the charity. They can only act on the lawful instructions of the

227

Charity Trustees and in accordance with any provisions contained in the governing document.

Some Questions relating to Trustees

How many Trustees must we have?

Under the Trustee Act 1925, and except where the Trustee is a Trust Company (a corporation), the minimum number of trustees for any charity is two and a trustee cannot resign without a replacement unless there will be at least two trustees left after the resignation.

While one cannot have fewer than two trustees, a minimum of three is obviously preferable, not least because of the problem if one dies or becomes incapacitated. Some church foundation deeds and constitutions specify a minimum number of deacons (trustees). This can sometimes be subject to amendment but it depends on the way the individual clauses are written.

It may also be thought that if an organisation cannot recruit three people willing to act as trustees then there are significant doubts as to the viability of that organisation.

If there were no Charity Trustees of the church, i.e. minister, named deacons, elders etc., then the legal position would appear to be that all the church members would be Charity Trustees. It is important that the Associations and other Custodian Trustees are sensitive to such a situation developing and are able to give the necessary support in good time (It is possible that some church members may not be able to act in this way being under eighteen, undischarged bankrupts or disqualified for some other reason from a trusteeship role).

While the Association or other Custodian Trustee should be kept informed it cannot "come in and take over or run" the church unless the church had closed, and then only in relation to property (not the church's working funds). Such bodies would have no legal authority to take action in relation to the working funds or accountability within the church.

So long as there is an active church, it is the responsibility of the members to arrange for the proper management of the charity by the appointment of Charity Trustees.

Private Trustees

Many churches have Denomination or Regional Trust Companies as their Custodian Trustees. There are still however a number of churches with private trustees. Any church with private trustees should know the names and addresses of their trustees that they are capable of serving in such office and are aware of their responsibilities. It is also suggested that this information be shared with the Regional Team. It is of course possible for the Private Custodian Trustees to request the Denomination or Regional Trust Company to take over trusteeship but this should be done in good time as the Trust Company could decline the offer if it reasonably felt that it would be loaded with unreasonable responsibilities, problems or financial risks.

Is the minister automatically a trustee and does that apply even if he is a student pastor, a non-recognised minister or a lay pastor?

Yes, a minister, or the senior minister if there is more than one, is automatically a trustee as they are involved in "the day to day management of the charity". This is related to the definition of a Charity Trustee in the 1993 Charities Act and is not something imposed in a Baptist (or other denomination) "rule book".

If in a group of small churches there are too few members willing and able to act as Charity Trustees, would it be possible for them to form/constitute/be classed as a trustee body for all the churches in that cluster?

It would be difficult to see how one group of Charity Trustees could be appointed to oversee the churches in that cluster. A church normally chooses its Charity Trustees from among its members and so a member of another church would not be qualified to act as a Managing Trustee from the outside.

It is however possible for a small group of churches, with compatible trust deeds, to unite to form one new church with several sites and congregations. This pattern should however only be used where there are a small number of churches within a definable community or locality. It should be the exception not the rule. It creates several advantages, including a better basis for the employment of a full time minister, the increased chance of a sufficient number of people being willing and able to serve as deacons and trustees, including some with leadership, organisational and financial skills and generally increased membership resources for the staffing of church organisations and, by no any means least, musical skills that might not be available in a smaller fellowship. It might also mean that the "combined" church could receive financial support for a minister, whereas the previously individual churches would not.

Can a Church delegate the job of Treasurer?

There is no reason why particular tasks such as accounting cannot be delegated to someone with the necessary skills and time, but this does not mean that the Charity Trustees have delegated accountability. All the Charity Trustees of the church are still accountable for overseeing the financial health of their charity, so in this instance they have simply asked somebody else to deal with day-to-day matters and produce the accounts for them. They must still scrutinise, check and approve the accounts. It is advisable for churches to appoint someone, whether from within the Leadership Team or general membership, to act as Secretary and someone else to act as Treasurer. Such people would automatically be Charity Trustees.

Funding

Funding is available for a range of work, from repairs on your church building, to an English as a Second Language class, to setting up a Parent and Toddler group. Before applying for funding, you must know if you want capital funding or revenue funding. For community projects, do a survey or audit of the area and discover the specific needs of your area before applying.

Euro-Funding

Available through the internet www.europeangrants.com mainly for areas of work across several countries, including teaming up with churches across Europe. Big regional projects also qualify for Euro-Funding. Each local government dept has a European office.

- Objective 1 funding – European social fund about employment and getting people ready to go back to work.
- Objective 2 funding – covers agriculture and rural areas.
- Objective 3 funding – national and local projects for needy areas.

However, 45% is given in Euro grants, 55% has to be found by the project, and the grant is paid in arrears. To qualify for Euro funds, 10% public funding has to be found.

Government Funding Streams

- Look at www.homeoffice.gov.uk and www.neighbourhood.gov.uk for ideas for local projects.
- There is a Regional Economic Strategy in every region. We as a church work both nationally and regionally, can we use our church buildings for the community as part of the area strategy?

Local Authority Grants

Global Grants for local communities range from £1000 to £10,000 – one-off grants for issues around life e.g. life skills, re-employment skills. Look at www.esf.gov.uk.

- "Connexions" for Youth can part-fund youth workers www.connexions-direct.com.
- Learning and Skills Council – training in Information Technology and other back-to-work skills, and they look for active local partners www.isc.gov.uk.

Lottery

Make up your own mind about lottery funding, but they give up to 75% grants to community projects. www.community-fund.org.uk. They give major funds, medium grants and Awards for All (small amounts but give them in about a month of applying).

Buildings

If there are old church buildings needing financial help, look at either:

> The Heritage Lottery Fund www.hlf.org.uk.
> Architectural Heritage Fund www.ahfund.org.uk.
> English Heritage www.english-heritage.org.uk.

Open Spaces

There is a fund, www.living-spaces.org.uk, to improve local spaces e.g. park, garden, church grounds etc. Grants of £1000 to £100,000 to support communities improving open spaces for all to use.

Trust Funds

These make direct grants for specific causes. See www.trustfunding.org.uk.

Do NOT send blanket letters to 300 trusts! They often have the same trustees – do your homework! Who are the trustees? What kind of causes do they send money to? Don't apply to the wrong trusts. Know how much to ask for. Target personally and be specific – make sure you know what you are asking for and why.

Working in the Community

Local Strategic Partnerships

Each LSP can have 2 faith representatives so find out who they are. The LSP works out a local community plan for the next 5 years.

THE COMPACT is the agreement between government and the voluntary and community sector in England to improve their relationship for mutual advantage. See the website www.thecompact.org.uk.

Baptist Union Guidelines available on www.baptist.org.uk or phone Baptist House 01235–517700 to order a paper copy.

East Dartmoor Baptist Church: Bovey Tracey – Chudleigh – Lustleigh – Moretonhampstead
A Community of Christians, Learning from Jesus and Sharing God's Love by Rev. Richard Starling, East Dartmoor Baptist Church

East Dartmoor Baptist Church (EDBC) is an example of local congregations coming together for mutual support, to share ministry, and to encourage mission. It witnesses to the eastern edge of Dartmoor and some of the congregations have a long history. Old Church Minutes reveal small but faithful groups seeking to serve Jesus under difficult circumstances.

During the 1970s, Bovey Tracey, Lustleigh and Moretonhampstead began to discuss a new vision. Because previous attempts to share ministry had been fruitless, they made a commitment to "get married" by forming one church membership with a combined church meeting, leadership team and budget. Later the congregations at Chudleigh and Christow joined EDBC.

How does East Dartmoor Baptist Church work?

Multiple congregations, even when they are trying to work as one church, have a different dynamic. It is not possible for the minister(s) to be a community figure in all locations, and there are restrictions on the time available in each congregation, even for preaching or leading worship. The church uses a team of local preachers and ministry is exercised as a team. There are currently two full-time ministers, three elders, and seven deacons to oversee the wider church; while local leadership deals with local issues within the village congregations. Larger congregations (Bovey and

Chudleigh) might normally expect to have their own ministers, but here they continue to share. Most "routine" pastoral care is done within the home groups, and it is possible for people to fall through the gaps. Since the church is aware of this, it puts great emphasis on caring for each other and being a friendly and supportive church. Usually, it works quite well!

While each congregation has faced its particular challenges, local initiatives keep up the momentum and the strength of the larger unit has helped enormously. This has been particularly true with regard to ministry, buildings and finance. EDBC would not claim to be a perfect solution and at times communication is complicated and making decisions can be slow, but against that, some of the smaller congregations would probably have closed if they had maintained their independence.

The generation that established EDBC was aware of their weakness and the new model offered hope in a series of difficult situations. However, the current generation does not remember those days, and the leadership have had to work hard at a vision to hold the church together.

Change is here to stay

East Dartmoor Baptist Church was originally set up with a pattern of local morning services and a joint evening service, open to all congregations, held at Bovey Tracey (the largest building). The aim was to unite the church and share a common vision through this combined service. Initially, it was the flagship teaching opportunity within the Church. In common with many other churches, attendance at evening worship has declined over the years. Travelling longish distances especially in winter evenings or through touring traffic can also be a deterrent. In response, the church established a new pattern and discovered the value of experimentation. Evenings now follow a new cycle: worship with communion, a prayer night, youth events, celebration-style worship, and "digging deeper" sessions (looking at biblical material, ethical questions, and current hot topics). Attendance varies, but is reasonable.

Different outcomes

Different congregations still have their own life and character. Bovey Tracey has always been the largest congregation, and continues to attract new people. It is a strong and lively group.

Moretonhampstead has been up and down numerically and finds maintaining a strong witness in a rural community difficult. This is also true in "picture postcard" Lustleigh, where faithfulness has maintained the chapel although numbers are small. Sadly, Christow eventually closed because there were no church members left living in the village.

In contrast, Chudleigh embarked on a "millennium re-launch" using the community hall and school. A new pattern of worship and mission was built on a foundation of prayer, supported by the rest of EDBC. Numbers have increased from 12 to 70, and a congregation with almost no children now thrives at the heart of its community.

Village life is not always hospitable to faith communities and shipping people in is only a short-term solution but East Dartmoor is in many ways a story of healthy creative tension, and an example of selfless mutual support. It will have to continually adapt to meet its changing situation and faces the challenge of how it can win new disciples in a village setting. It also raises the questions; can "church" be trans-denominational and can we constructively combine Baptist ways of "doing church" (ecclesiology) with Anglican rural tradition?

Some people prefer to travel to the larger towns and congregations rather than get involved in a small chapel. Yet, where communities are developing, it has been possible to grow a vibrant congregation with increasing opportunities for church planting. At least two local villages do not have an effective Christian presence; it may be that new congregations and/or homegroups can be established via EDBC.

The Dream

The church has a dream of being a church of 500 members, worshipping and witnessing throughout south Devon, being a resource to other Christian churches in the area and being a sending church, involved in mission and practical love throughout the world.

To achieve this, it must be flexible whilst holding on to its core values and Christ based foundation. The aim is to help its members to be positive witnesses, attractive in their faith and character, and so able to help others find living faith in Christ. Only the Holy Spirit can turn the dream into reality.

RESOURCES

These resources are listed by chapter heading and all details were correct at the time of going to print.

Worship

Music
CDs and DVDs.
Good selection at your local Christian Bookshop or at Wesley Owen (telephone 0800 834315; www.wesleyowen.com)
Integrity Music (telephone 0845 055 6056; www.integrityeurope.com)

Song books/music books/hymn books – Songs of Fellowship
Your local Christian bookshop or Kingsway Communications (telephone 01323 437755; www.equippingthechurch.co.uk)

Midi hymnal
No organist or music group? – No problem; Self-playing organ or CD series with backing tracks.
DM Music (telephone 0500 026930; www.dmmusic.com)

Small Church Music
Good quality accompaniments for congregational singing available at no cost.
(www.smallchurchmusic.com)

Kevin Mayhew Publishers
Christian books and music.
No Music Group? No Problem – set of 200 favourite songs and hymns backing tracks.
Kevin Mayhew (telephone 01449 737978 for a catalogue; www.kevinmayhew.com)

DM Music for Churches
Books/CDs and equipment from microphones to keyboards.
DM Music (telephone 0500 026930; www.dmmusic.com)

Church Copyright Licensing (Europe) Ltd
Copyright Licences for reproducing a song on a screen, printed on paper or recorded; photocopying music; showing videos/DVDs; recording weddings etc. on video/digital cameras.
CCLI, Chantry House, 22 Upperton Road, Eastbourne BN21 1BF (telephone 01323 436100; www.ccli.co.uk)

Resource books
Ideas for All Age Worship and *Alternative Worship Activities.*
(Your local Christian Bookshop)

London Baptist Association Preachers Database
A database of available Baptist preachers across London.
Database Manager – Neil Tresise (telephone 0208 977 1279; E-mail neiltresise@hotmail.com)

Discipleship

Freedom in Christ
Leader's Guide, Participant's Guide and other resources.
Freedom in Christ (telephone 0118 988 8173; www.ficm. org.uk)

Ellel Ministries
Centre offering days, weekends and longer residential training courses. Subjects include healing, freedom from depression or addiction.
Ellel Ministries (telephone 01252 794060; www.ellelministries. co.uk)

Word and Spirit Resources
Books, teaching and courses led by Rev. Mark Stibbe, J. John and others.

Wordandspiritminstries.org.uk – St Andrews Church, Chorley-wood Herts (telephone 01923 447 7111; www.st-andrews.org.uk)

Waverley Christian Training
Waverley Abbey Brochure contains details of counselling and other courses.
Waverley Christian Training at CWR (telephone 01252 784700; www.cwr.org.uk)

Every Day with Jesus; Every Day with Jesus for New Christians
Daily Bible readings
Available from Your local Christian bookshop.

Purpose Driven
Strategic and discipleship tools and programmes.
Purpose Driven UK (telephone 01255 435577; www.purpose-driven. co.uk)

Emmaus Course
Discipleship Bible study course
Church House Publishing (telephone 0207 898 1451; www. e-mmaus.org.uk)

Lifewords (formerly Scripture Gift Mission)
Tracts and Tools for Mission.
Lifewords (telephone 0207 730 2155; www.lifewords.info)

Lifebuilder Bible Series
Bible study guides for small groups.
Scripture Union (telephone 01908 865000; www.scriptureunion. org.uk)
Available from your local Christian bookshop.

Time for Each Other
Marriage Course.

Christian Publishing and Outreach – CPO (telephone 01903 263354; E-mail sales@cpo.org.uk; www.cpo.org.uk)

Wesley Owen – for software, books, CDs
Provides Bible study software, commentary, clip art etc: SongPro – worship software; Cashcall – software for treasurers.
Wesley Owen (telephone 0800 834315; www.wesleyowen.com)

United Christian Broadcasters, Europe
Prayerline, Radio, TV, UCB Mobile, Looking for God, Word for Today, UCB2GO, UCB Aid.
UCB (telephone 0845 6040401; www.ucb.co.uk)

Baptist/Baptism
Who'd be a Baptist?, *Baptism and Belonging.*
Baptist Union Publications (telephone 01235 517743; www.baptiststore.co.uk)

Life Course
Life Course, Whose life is it anyway? (Life Course for youth), Growth Course.
Christian Publishing and Outreach – CPO (telephone 01903 263354; E-mail sales@cpo.org.uk; www.cpo.org.uk)

Recommended books/CDs
Pure by Linda Marshall (Boy/Girl Relationships course);
10 Qualities of a Healthy Small Group by Rick Warren and Tom Halladay.
Available from your local Christian Bookshop

Fellowship

Recommended Books
Special Church, Special Needs by Simon Bass ISBN 0 7151 4999 7.
Church House Publishing.

Book for the 18–30s age group
   Ctrl:Alt:Del by the Baptist Union Young Leaders Forum.
   Baptist Union Publications (telephone 01235 517743; www.
   baptiststore.co.uk)

Healthy Church UK
   Resources for healthy churches with resources for smaller
   churches.
   Healthy Church UK (telephone 01767 692938; www.healthychurch.
   co.uk)

Urban Expression
   Creative church planting in the inner city.
   www.UrbanExpression.org.uk; enquiries@urbanexpression.org.
   uk

Christians struggling with sexuality issues
   Annual conferences and support, help and encouragement.
   True Freedom Trust (telephone 0151 653 0773; www.
   truefreedomtrust.co.uk)

Training for Churches (Baptist)
   TiMM Course run by Northern Baptist College in the
   Midlands.
   www.northern.org.uk/html/working_with_churches.html
   DELTA Courses run by Regents Park College or Bristol College.
   www.rpc.ox.ac.uk; www.bristol-baptist.ac.uk

Training for Churches (Methodist)
   Training and Development Officer.
   Methodist Church House (telephone 0207 486 5502)

Mission

Recommended Books
>   *Sowing, Reaping, Keeping* by Laurence Singlehurst;
>   *50 Ways to Help your Church Grow* by David Beer;
>   *Reaching People, the Small Church Approach* by Dan Yarnell;
>   *Dinner with a Perfect Stranger* by David Gregory.
>   Available from your Local Christian Bookshop

Home Mission (Baptist)
>   Grants are available to facilitate mission in any size of church.
>   Contact your Regional Association

Mission Resources (Methodist)
>   Funding and other resources
>   Central Building, Oldham Street, Manchester, M1 1JQ (telephone
>   0161 236 5194)

FEBV – Fellowship for Evangelising Britain's Villages
>   Can settle evangelists within an existing church and produces
>   prayer letter for smaller churches.
>   Peter Smith (telephone 01823 321016; www.febv.org.uk)

On the Move Missions
>   Town or area wide mission with barbecue.
>   (Telephone 0121 427 3300; www.onthemove.org.uk)

Urban Expression
>   Help with church planting and emerging church in urban and
>   inner city settings.
>   Urban Expression (www.urbanexpression.org.uk)

Outreach to Muslims
>   London based Arabic Christian Centre and "how to share your
>   faith with Muslims" training.
>   Agapé Arabic Christian Centre (telephone 0207 221 4355)

The Reachout Trust
  Equipping the church to build bridges to people in the cults, the
  occult and other faiths.
  The Reachout Trust (telephone 0870 770 3258; www.
  reachouttrust.org)

Green Shoots
  Funding for new mission initiatives within Baptist Churches.
  Your Regional Minister

*Alpha Course, Senior Alpha, Student Alpha, Youth Alpha, Alpha
for prisons, Alpha for forces, Alpha in the work place*
  Introduction to Christianity course materials
  Available from your Local Christian Bookshop

Christianity Explored
  Introduction to Christianity course
  Wesley Owen (telephone 0800 834315; www.wesleyowen.com)

Y Course
  Introduction to Christianity course
  Christian Publishing and Outreach – CPO (telephone 01903
  263354; E-mail sales@cpo.org.uk; www.cpo.org.uk)

Jesus Video Project
  A project for the widespread distribution of a video about Jesus.
  sales@agape.org.uk (telephone 0121 765 4404; www.agape.org.
  uk/jvp)

The Contagious Christian course
  Willow Creek resource by Bill Hybels.
  Available from your local Christian Bookshop

10+ (study guides and DVD)
  10 commandments study guide

PhiloTrust (telephone 01923 287777; www.philotrust.com)

Books on relationships
Marriage and Being Single
PhiloTrust (telephone 01923 287777; www.philotrust.com)

Study guides
The Lord's Prayer study guide
PhiloTrust (telephone 01923 287777; www.philotrust.com)

Viz-a-Viz
Reaching adults, children, young people and equipping the church.
Viz-a-Viz (telephone 01268 530531; www.vizaviz.org)

Leadership

Consultancy Programme
A small team of consultants can facilitate vision/mission in your church.
Your Regional Minister (Baptist); District Superintendent (Methodist)

Home Mission Grant (Baptist)
Part or full-time leaders can be part funded.
Your Regional Minister

Funding for Methodist Churches
Circuit Advanced Funds; District Advanced Funds.
Contact your Circuit or District Superintendent

BUild
Baptist Union initiative for people with learning difficulties. Advice and literature available.
Baptist Union (telephone 01235 517700; www.baptist.org.uk)

Church Pastoral Aid Society
Evangelism for youth and children; Arrow Leadership Programme; Growing Leaders Course.
CPAS (telephone 01926 458458; www.cpas.org.uk)

Recommended Books
Freedom to Lead by Colin Buckland (CWR);
How to Thrive as a Small Church Pastor by Steve R Bierly;
Small Church, Big Vision by Lynn Green and Chris Forster;
Nothing spiritual about chaos by Rachel Tole.
Baptist Union Publications (www.baptiststore.co.uk)
And available from your local Christian Bookshop

Safe to Belong
Vulnerable adult resources from the Baptist Union.
Baptist Union (telephone 01235 517700; www.baptist.org.uk)

Children and Young People

Light from Scripture Union
This and similar publications contain ready-planned "Sunday School" sessions.
Scripture Union (telephone 01908 856000; www.scriptureunion. org.uk)

Holiday Club materials
Ready planned Holiday Club activities.
Available from your local Christian bookshop

Beginners Bible videos
Series of videos covering major Bible stories in cartoon format.
www.integrityeurope.com; telephone 0845 055 6056
And available from your local Christian bookshop

Children's Ministry
Annual Conference for Children's workers; produce Sunday School materials.
www.childrensministry.co.uk; e-mail childrensministry@ kingsway.co.uk; telephone 01323 437 748

Care for the Family
Books, conferences, events and newsletters for Mums, Dads and Families.
Care for the Family (telephone 0292 081 0800; www.careforthe-family.org.uk)

Safe to Grow
Child protection resources from the Baptist Union.
Baptist Union (telephone 01235 517700; www.baptist.org.uk)

The Churches' Child Protection Advisory Service
Provides literature and up to date training for all areas of child protection and good working practice; courses on DVD.
CCPAS (telephone 01322 667207; www.ccpas.co.uk; www. childprotection.net)

CURBS
Works with a wide range of inner city and urban children. Provides materials for clubs etc. and training; fosters spiritual development in a child relevant and Biblical way.
Mrs Kathryn Copsey (telephone 07941 336589; www.curbsproject. org.uk)

Christian Education
Provides resources for churches using *Teddy Horsley* for the under 5s; series of books for Youth Work – *Roots*; allocates small grants to subscriber churches for residential youth work.
Christian Education (telephone 0121 472 4242; www.christiane-ducation.org.uk; www.christianeducation.org.uk/roots.htm)

Go Teach
Bible teaching resources
Go Teach (telephone 01625 422272; www.goteach.org.uk)

Youth for Christ
Youth Workers and Resources for Youth Work.
Youth for Christ (telephone 0121 550 8055; www.yfc.co.uk)

Youth Resources
Website and regular magazines, books and annual conference.
www.youthwork.co.uk

Barnabas
Resources for children's work in church and schools.
www.barnabasinchurches.org.uk

Bible Reading Fellowship
Not Sunday! Not School! By E. Zuercher, ISBN 1 84191 490 7.
BRF Publishing (telephone 01865 319700)

Funding for Youth Projects
Type "Youth Funding" into the internet search engine to find many sources of funding.

Recommended Books
Where two or three . . . by Margaret Withers;
Children and Bereavement by Wendy Duffy;
Not Just Sunday by Margaret Withers;
Mission Shaped Children by Margaret Withers.
Church House Publishing

Partnership

Small Churches Network
In some Baptist Associations
Your Regional Minister

Baptist Union of Great Britain
National resource for the Baptist denomination.
Baptist House, 129 Broadway, Didcot, OX11 8RT (telephone 01235 517700; www.baptist.org.uk)

Churches Together in England
Ecumenical body encouraging working together.
Churches Together in England (telephone 0207 529 8131; www.churches-together.org.uk)

The Methodist Church
National resource for the Methodist denomination.
Methodist Church House, 25 Marylebone Road, London NW1 1JR (telephone 0207 486 5502; www.methodistchurch.org.uk)

247 Network
A network of churches committed to working together and separately to the vision statement "Favour and Growth".
247 Network (tim.heard@w3z.co.uk; www.twofortyseven.net)

Evangelical Alliance
Alliance for evangelical Christians in the UK across 30 denominations and organisations, and individuals.
Evangelical Alliance (telephone 0207 207 2100; www.eauk.org)

Arthur Rank Centre
Organisation supporting the rural community and its churches.
ARC (telephone 02476 853060; www.arthurrankcentre.org.uk)

Rural Missions
Organisation resourcing small, rural churches including: REN – Rural Evangelism Network – a forum for the sharing of insight and experience in rural mission; Rural Sunrise – helps rural churches to engage in mission; East Midlands Rural Mission Partnership.

Rural Missions, 4 Clarence Street, Market Harborough, Leics LE16 7NE (telephone 01858 414930; www.ruralmissions.org.uk)

Hands-on Help booklet (for anyone in a small church)
To encourage and help small churches in their mission by finding people to help with specific tasks.
Contact your local Baptist Association Office.

Freecycling
An internet-based system, organised regionally, to exchange no-longer-wanted goods at no cost.
www.freecycle.org

Against the Stream
Funding for projects for Baptist Churches working to combat community poverty.
Available from your Regional Minister

Local Council Advisor on funding for charity and community organisations
There may be a local council employee who can tell you which organisations you could apply to and help you to make the application.
Contact your Local Council

Buildings

Peter Stockwell (based in Chichester)
Advice/consultations on building and legal matters.
Telephone 01243 839801; e-mail: prb.stockwell@virgin.net

Church Purchasing Scheme
Catalogue of church equipment available to buy.
CPS (telephone 0845 458 4584; www.cpsonline.co.uk)

Baptist Building Fund
   Your local Association
   Regional Minister

Baptist Strategy Building Fund
   Your local Association
   Regional Minister

Other Legal and Regulatory

Baptist Union Corporation Guidelines
   Advice from the Corporation manager. Available online and by post.
   Telephone 01235 517745; www.baptist.org.uk

Charity Commission for England and Wales
   Advice and downloadable information relating to Charity governance and Trustee matters.
   Charity Commission Direct, PO Box 1227, Liverpool L69 3UG (telephone 0870 30000218; www.charity-commission.gov.uk)

Solicitors
   Expensive advice but sometimes necessary!
   Local recommendation

Other

The Baptist Times
   Various stories of life in Baptist churches around the world, news and letters.
   The Baptist Times (telephone 01235 517672; www.baptisttimes. co.uk)

The Methodist Recorder
   Various stories of life in Methodist churches around the world, news and letters.

The Methodist Recorder (telephone 0207 251 8414; www. methodistrecorder.co.uk)

The Church Times
Various stories of life in Anglican churches around the world, news and letters.
The Church Times (telephone 0207 359 4570; www.churchtimes. co.uk)

Christian Resources Exhibition
Exhibition with lots of ideas and suppliers held in various locations.
CRE (www.creonline.co.uk)

Christian Centres and Camps

Barnabas Adventure Centres
Youth Adventure Centres in Kent, Northants and Scottish Borders
Barnabas Adventure Centres Ltd (telephone 01732 366766; www.barnabas.org.uk)

High Leigh – Herts; The Hayes – Derbys
Retreat/conference centres.
Christian Conference Trust (www.cct.org.uk)

Spring Harvest (registered charity)
Lively Easter breaks at Butlins sites at Skegness and Minehead.
Spring Harvest, 14 Horsted Square, E.Sussex TN22 1QG (telephone 01825 769000; e-mail info@springharvest.org; www. springharvest.org)

New Wine
Lively summer camps and much more.
New Wine (telephone 0208 567 6717; www.new-wine.org)

Leading Edge
> Lively family camp run by the Baptist Union.
> Leading Edge (telephone 01235 517752; www.baptist.org.uk/ leadingedge)

Oak Hall
> Ski/snowboard or summer holidays; Bible or Mission weekends; Short-term mission abroad.
> Oak Hall (telephone 01732 763131; www.oakhall.co.uk)

The Society of Mary and Martha
> Retreat centre for tired ministers.
> The Society of Mary and Martha, Dunsford, Exeter, Devon (telephone 01647 252752; www.sheldon.uk.com)

Christian Entertainers

One Way UK
> Puppets.
> One Way UK (telephone 0118 975 6303; www.onewayuk.com)

Jim Bailey and Kingdom Creative
> Children's Gospel fun with songs, puppets and teachers training sessions.
> Kingdom Creative (telephone 01903 522627; www.jimbailey.org)

The Still Time Band
> Jazz for any occasion.
> The Still Time Band (telephone 0208 8441637; www.stilltime. com)

APPENDIX

S.W.O.T. ANALYSIS IN THE NEW TESTAMENT

The Letters to the Seven Churches – by Martin Taylor, Ashford Common Baptist Church

When I first thought about applying a SWOT (Strengths, Weaknesses, Opportunities, Threats) Analysis to a church, I wasn't over keen. Management tools like SWOT have their place in the world, but is it really appropriate to use them in a spiritual context? Should we take the world and works of man and apply them to God's world. There are a good number of Christians who would count that as being of the Devil! And yet, it does seem a very logical thing to do. Work out what, as a Church you are good at and bad at. Think through what doors are opening, and what problems are looming. It focuses the mind so well on what is important.

Clearly, it could all go wrong. People could just play at it and not come up with serious answers. There might be no consensus on what needed attention. It might drag up some dirty washing that we didn't want to see in public. But most of all, it wasn't right simply to impose a management technique on an unsuspecting church.

Then my wife directed me to a tape by Rev. Mark Stibbe on the letters to the churches in Revelation. Mark described how each of the seven letters had seven sections. Mark didn't use quite the same headings as I am about to, nor was his aim to draw a conclusion about SWOT. But it was enough to set me thinking.

However, I can't just hand it to you on a plate, you have to work at this to appreciate how God works. So open your Bibles to

253

Revelation chapter 2. The Letter to the Church at Pergamum, starts at verse 12. The pattern is most clearly laid out here. The first two of the seven sections are in verse 12 – a signature and an address. Most letters tell you who they are to and most tell you who they are from. And these letters are no exception. The author of each and every letter is Jesus, and in verse 12, the letter is addressed to the Angel of the Church in Pergamum.

Two down, five to go. Let's look now at verse 13. The sort of things Jesus is saying here are all positive. So in terms of a SWOT Analysis they would be Strengths.

In verses 14 and 15 Jesus is exposing their Weaknesses. Next in a SWOT analysis? Opportunities! Can you see an opportunity outlined in the first couple of words of verse 16? Repent! Yes indeed. What greater opportunity could face any of us?

What can you find in the rest of the verse? Yes, the "Or else" does rather give it away. It is a clear Threat.

And there you have it. Strengths, Weaknesses, Opportunities, Threats. The Apostle John got the hang of SWOT analysis 2000 years before the management consultants caught up. Who says the Bible is not up to date?

Oh, wait a minute, I hear you cry. You have only covered six out of the seven points that you promised. What about the last one? OK, let's look at verse 17. How would you describe that? I agree, it does look a bit like an opportunity. I'd like to put a different angle on it though. The opportunities you will find in the Letters to the Churches are all fairly immediate. The things that occur at the end of each letter are more futuristic. I think a better way of describing them is a Promise. He who overcomes will . . . And isn't that just typical of our God? He doesn't just leave us with what mankind would dump on us. He always has something good held out to us. He always looks to the positive. He lavishes His promises upon us.

Now of course, John wasn't writing a management treatise, and so his letters aren't quite laid out perfectly to fit my taxonomy. So I need to point out where the statements are not quite in "my" order. The order is much clearer if you are able to set the letters out in a table with lines to delineate where the various sections should start and finish (see example below). In the letter to Ephesus, Rev 2v6 probably fits better under the Strengths heading. The Letter to Smyrna has no Weaknesses, and no Threats. There is probably a sermon in there about the linkage between threats and weaknesses. I have counted the expectation of persecution as an opportunity – though they themselves might have disagreed at the time.

In the Letter to Thyatira, Rev 2v21–23 is really Threat material though it occurs before rather than after the Opportunities. The Letter to Sardis is not very complimentary. The only items that could really count as Strengths occur in Rev 3v4 instead of in the expected place, which is the middle of verse 1.

The Letter to Philadelphia is short of specific Strengths, though one gets the impression that Jesus is pleased. Rev 3v8 could be cut different ways. I have chosen to split it between Strengths and Weaknesses. This Letter also has no discernible Threats.

Finally, the Letter to Laodicea has no Strengths at all. Their worldly Strengths – riches and wealth – Jesus clearly regards as major weaknesses. So much so that the Threat comes in Rev 3v16 rather than between verses 20 and 21.

Please turn to page 256 to see this illustrated in tabular form.

If you find pictures and patterns easier to understand then the following exercise might make this easier. Take 2 sheets of A4 paper (or a word processor equivalent) and set them out as follows. Insert the full text where the verses are shown. The arrows show where the italicised verses need to be moved from → to to slot them into the order for a SWOT test.

To	2v1a	2v8a	2v12a
From	2v1b	2v8b	2v12b
Strengths	2v2, 3	2v9	2v13
Weaknesses	2v4		2v14, 15
Opportunities	2v5a	2v10	2v16a
Threats	2v5b		2v16b
Promise	2v6 / 2v7	2v11	2v17

To	2v18a	3v1a	3v7a	3v14a
F	2v18b	3v1b	3v7b	3v14b
S	2v19		3v8a	
W	2v20, 21 / 2v22, 23	3v1c	3v8b	3v15 / 3v16 / 3v17
O	2v24, 25	3v2, 3a	3v9–11	3v18–20
T		3v3b		
P	2v26–29	3v4 / 3v5, 6	3v12, 13	3v21, 22